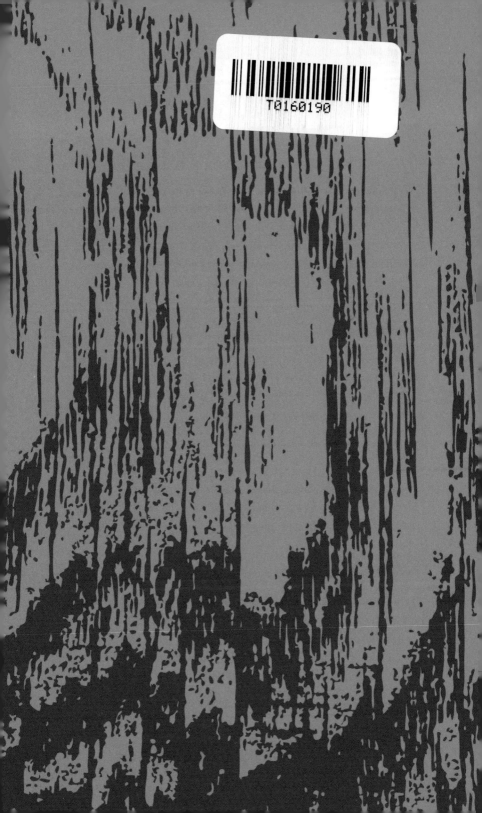

# Praise for *Mother Nature Is Not Trying to Kill You*

"You might never be stung by a Portuguese man o' war or chased by a polar bear. But it doesn't matter. The Nelsons will have you hooked as he weaves stories with facts from what seems like every corner of the earth. His book is an awesome gathering of fascinating survival tips and practical advice for anyone who steps outdoors. Knots, shelters, knives, and animal attacks...need I say more?!"

—**Chris Morgan**, National Geographic explorer, TV host, and bear biologist

"This is a must-have for any budding biologists, wildlife lovers, or future nature-show hosts! I wish I had this book when I was growing up and plan on stealing my kids' copy of it to serve as a quick reference guide for future adventures!"

—**Pat Spain**, National Geographic biologist for *Beast Hunter*

"This is exactly what I needed as a kid and now it acts as a great reference. I make a living as a survival expert I can verify this is THE BEST info out there now on these wild plants and animals. It's fun to read and accessible for all audiences."

—**Hazen Audel**, survival expert and host of National Geographic's *Primal Survivor*

"What a great book! The Nelsons expertly blend fascinating wildlife and nature facts and serious wilderness survival techniques with a healthy dose of fun and humor. Even if you'll never face any of these animals or survival situations in real life, you'll learn a lot and be entertained no matter what your age."

—**David Mizejewski**, naturalist, National Wildlife Federation

"The Nelsons say mother nature is not out to kill you, and they should know. They've given her many, many chances. Part survival guide, part science lesson, and part campfire story, this book provides an entertaining look at dozens of ways people can die in the wild. Rob and Haley dig into the facts behind each of these threats and provide practical advice for surviving them. It's an engaging and educational read for nature-lovers of all ages."

—**Nick Whitney**, shark biologist, New England Aquarium

"Listen. If I were to be stranded in the wilderness, there's nothing I'd rather have with me than Rob and Haley. But carrying two full grown adults would be A LOT of weight for the ol' backpack, so I'm uber stoked that they've condensed their survival brains into this incredible, easily transportable book."

—**Dustin Growick**, science communicator extraordinaire, DinosaurWhisperer

"A captivating read full of useful tips on how to enjoy and interact with nature while avoiding troublesome encounters with wild animals. It provides a balanced, commonsense perspective of 'dangerous' wildlife from bears to sharks, mosquitoes to jellyfish, and is peppered with delightfully quirky illustrations! Written in an engaging style, this fascinating and informative book will be a great addition to any nature buff's library."

—**Dave Abbott**, Sharkweek cameraman

"Part 'what if?' guide, part survival book, part fact-packed treasure trove about the wild and its wildlife! I would have loved to have this book as a kid! Such an engaging read, packed with top-tips from the authors' close-encounters with the wild and its wildlife. Just brilliant."

—**Greg Foot**, science broadcaster, BBC

"A captivating book for anyone who is scared of nature; The Nelsons use science and experience to demystify the animals that cause fear in people while providing advice on how to deal with potentially dangerous situations."

—**Gaelin Rosenwaks**, marine biologist, The Explorers Club

"Rob's life experiences have taught him not to fear nature but to respect and admire its power from afar—when you can. When you can't, this is the book to help you navigate those rare moments, all while learning and appreciating the wild and wonderful world around us. My heart's still pounding from the sailboat story and now I want to feed a piranha goldfish."

—**Phil Torres**, *ExpeditionX* scientist, Discovery Channel

"Informative, entertaining, and relatable, all in one book."

—**Dr. Casey Parker**, mosquito biologist, University of Florida

"As a scientist, I've relied on Rob's experience and advice for how to tell stories about the natural world. Now he's brought his experience and advice together for an expert, honest, and entertaining guide to interacting with nature. And it's excellent!"

—**Dr. Adrian Smith**, entomologist, NC State University

"Highly recommend! This book, written in easily-understandable and thoroughly entertaining language, is an entertaining read even for someone who doesn't like nature, and Rob's use of personal stories and anecdotes keeps the reader glued to the pages."

—**Dr. David Coyle**, biologist, Clemson SC

"The natural world often gets bad press, most of which is not deserved. Rob and Haley have done an amazing job dispelling some of the great wildlife myths. This a welcome addition to anyone's book collection!"

—**David Bodenham**, ecologist, eco sapien

"For any outdoor explorer, the personal experiences that Rob shares in this guide should be as important a take-along as water, bug spray, and a good map. Even if you don't plan to come face-to-face with a water buffalo any time soon, the personal experiences in this guide will help prepare you for all kinds of outdoor (mis) adventures."

—**Jim Brady**, biologist

"A great book, full of interesting and fun facts about our not-so-dangerous housemates on planet earth."

—**Dr. Damien Caillaud**, Professor of Anthropology, UC Davis

"Our understanding of nature has been hampered for centuries by myths and misinformation guided mostly by fear. In this book, the Nelsons take a different approach than most others, by using both science and entertainment to help us gain a better understanding of the species humans fear the most and provide tips, should you ever be lucky enough to encounter one of these species. In addition to providing some of their own scientific knowledge, the species accounts were reviewed and edited by experts and researchers from around the world. The stories, images, and graphics are unique and help make this light-hearted survival guide worth the read."

—**Dustin Smith**, herpetologist, NC Zoo

"Wild pig attacks on humans are rare, but can be deadly. Rob Nelson's advice can keep you safe when it comes to these pigs."

—**Dr. John Mayer**, biologist, wild boar expert

"I'm always looking for books that broaden the scope of tone and topic to more fully engage my students, so as an educator and an amateur wildlife enthusiast, I love the gap that this book fills when it comes to lively wilderness survival. This book is a welcomed reawakening to students whose reading lists are all-too-commonly bogged down with outdated and boring topics, and it speaks to the vivid, inquisitive type of biology that kids are used to before we steal it away to hand them a common core textbook. From the perspective of an English teacher, it feels like the *Into the Wild* that Chris McCandless wishes he could have lived to write."

—**April Noethe Wolford**, highschool english teacher, Sparta, Wisconsin

"In a world that too often attempts to entertain with sensationalism and hype, Rob and Haley's new book offers a refreshing blend of science, reality, and common sense on interacting with the interesting wildlife that shares our planet. But perhaps the biggest reward of reading this book is that it will absolutely make you a smarter and more sensible person who, in turn, can safely explore the wild or inspire creative conversations about all the nature craft and interesting biology you'll learn within the pages. So in the end, this book delivers what few others can...it will actually make your life richer in both knowledge and how to confidently embrace our great outdoors."

—**Dan Bertalan**, award-winning author of *Nature Comes Killing*

"Listen to Rob and Haley when it comes to close encounters with nature and wildlife. Their book takes the right approach: gathering the facts and presenting them in a fun way so the reader can make their own decisions when it comes to interacting with the wild."

—**Greg Weiss**, survival instructor

"The Nelsons have mastered the art of storytelling in short science videos, and now bring their artistry to book form on a topic that everyone should pay attention to—how not to get eaten!"

—**Dr. Roland Kays**, Director of Biodiversity, Museum of Natural Sciences

"Wow! This is a book every young adventurer should have in their collection. Rob Nelson's ability to make science sound like a casual conversation makes this a fun, breezy, exhilarating and informative collection of some of the world's most charismatic and feared animals. Having this book in your backpack just may save your life one day."

—**Jesse Weiland**, National Park Ranger

"I spend my life in remote places and have see people do incredible things and live a full life. I've also seen people put their hand inside a volcano and recoil in surprise that it was hot. Both of these types of people can glean something from this book. Well-written and beautifully illustrated, putting fact before fiction with survival scenarios."

—**Huw James**, adventurer

"A witty and informative guide on how not to die in nature. An informative book filled with fun anecdotes from the author to soften to blow."

—**Neil Gonzalez**, wildlife photographer

"I absolutely loved this book! It's a great introduction to wild animals that my boys think of as 'dangerous.' We learned lots of new facts and survival strategies, and stimulated our imagination with 'what ifs.' The illustrations brought lots of giggles and lightened what could be seen as a scary or intense subject matter. The authors' own life experiences and stories make the book feel personal, like we're all sitting around a fire regaling tales from our youth. The book is funny, fascinating, and packed full of useful information and tips. It reads like a series of short stories that are chock full of useful information. My family is looking forward to diving deeper into our favorite subjects that we were introduced to—bison for the little ones, and piranhas for the big kid. Thank you, authors, for planting a seed of wonder and a thirst for knowledge in my boys!"

—**Ashley Grice**, YMCA's youth director

"A perfect mix of entertainment, real science, and dinner table fun facts!"

—**Jonas Stenstrom**, award winning filmmaker, *UntamedScience*

"Saying that *Mother Nature Is Not Trying to Kill You* made me want to swim in piranha-filled rivers sounds like a bad thing, but it's actually a great one! In taking the mystery and media-frenzy out of some of the most interesting animals in the world, Rob and Haley Nelson tell you what to do and what not to do when faced with nature's power. With clear explanations, exciting anecdotes, and real-world stories of coexisting with Mother Nature, this book gives you the knowledge and confidence to explore and enjoy the beauty of the planet and its animal inhabitants, without accidentally winding up as lunch!"

—**Dr. Alex Dainis**, biologist, YouTuber

"This book grabs you from the get-go! The unique combination of facts and storytelling makes for an informative and entertaining read. You won't want to put this one down!"

—**ChimneySwift11**, YouTuber, amature bushcrafter

"A fascinating book filled with fascinating insights into the plants and animals we inhabit this world with a definite must-have for any outdoorsman's library. *Mother Nature* makes the world less scary, but certainly more interesting! The threat of seemingly unpredictable wildlife in the woods can be a constant fear, but this book goes a long way to ease that; I wish I'd read it sooner!"

—**Peter Forrester**, survival instructor

"FINALLY! As a huge fan of Rob and Haley's work, I had to absorb what I could through their social media platforms and Science Channel collaborations... So you could imagine how stoked I was when this book released. It definitely did not disappoint. Remember when you were a kid and would reread your favorite 'fun facts' book over and over again? Well, this is the big kid version. Entertaining. Full of info. And a pure joy to read... And reread."

—**Mallory Lindsay**, wildlife guide, TV host

"Listen. Do you ever wonder, *How would I live through a bear encounter?* Do you want to know how to survive a crocodile attack? Of course you do. Rob and Haley have collected knowledge in this book that was hard won by people who suffered so you don't have to. Read this. Learn from it. Survive. I once found myself within arms distance of a black bear. In moments like those, you realize how little you know. I wish I'd found this book sooner!"

—**Nick Householder**, scientist, Midnight Science Club

"*Mother Nature is Not Trying to Kill You* is a fantastic guide for how to stay safe around some of our planet's most remarkable creatures. Free from hype, it neither over nor under exaggerates the dangers posed by wild animals or plants, but states the facts for what they are. Equal parts funny and practical, this book could literally save your life."

—**Josh Gross**, archeologist, Americorp

"If you love wildlife and the great outdoors, this book is for you, exciting and filled with wonderful facts about potentially dangerous animals. Nature sometimes can be unpredictable, and this book is the perfect, simple guide to understanding wildlife and what to do if you ever have a close encounter with a wild animal. A captivating and enjoyable mixture of science, adventure and storytelling about nature. It's essential reading for everyone who wants to understand nature, wildlife, and wants to be prepared for a 'just in case' situation."

In spanish (*en español*): "Si te gusta la vida silvestre y las actividades al aire libre, este libro es para ti, emocionante y lleno de hechos maravillosos sobre animales potencialmente peligrosos. La naturaleza a veces puede ser impredecible, y este libro es la perfecta y simple guía para entender la vida silvestre y qué hacer si alguna vez tienes un encuentro cercano con un animal salvaje. Una cautivadora y agradable mezcla de ciencia, aventura y narración de historias sobre la naturaleza. Es una lectura esencial para todo aquel que quiera entender la naturaleza, la vida silvestre, y quiera estar preparado para cualquier situación 'por si acaso.'"

—**Sofia Villalpando**, biologist (*biologista*)

"I'm proud to say that this book was written by my son-in-law and daughter. Their adventurous life together has always encouraged others to enjoy the wild natural world—but always in a safe way. May you be inspired by the valuable information within to explore and appreciate even the scary parts of nature!"

—**Ann Chamberlain**, family therapist

# MOTHER NATURE IS NOT TRYING TO KILL YOU

# MOTHER NATURE IS NOT TRYING TO KILL YOU

## A WILDLIFE & BUSHCRAFT SURVIVAL GUIDE

### ROB NELSON & HALEY NELSON

mango
PUBLISHING GROUP

CORAL GABLES

Cover Design: Elina Diaz
Cover Photo/Illustration: stock.adobe.com/SlothAstronaut
Interior Illustrations: Rob Nelson, stock.adobe.com
Layout & Design: Elina Diaz

For permission requests, please contact the publisher at:
Mango Publishing Group
2850 S Douglas Road, 2nd Floor
Coral Gables, FL 33134 USA
info@mango.bz

For special orders, quantity sales, course adoptions and corporate sales, please email the publisher at sales@mango.bz. For trade and wholesale sales, please contact Ingram Publisher Services at customer.service@ingramcontent.com or +1.800.509.4887.

Mother Nature Is Not Trying to Kill You: A Wildlife & Bushcraft Survival Guide

Library of Congress Cataloging-in-Publication number: 2020940955
ISBN: (print) 978-1-64250-321-0, (ebook) 978-1-64250-322-7
BISAC category code: REF031000—REFERENCE / Survival & Emergency Preparedness

Printed in the United States of America

To our boys, August and Leo, who are growing up in a world that is changing way too fast. May you learn to stay grounded in the wilder things of this world—using those brains and hearts of yours to be smart, be safe, and protect the real-life magic of nature.

# Table of Contents

# It May Happen One Day—It Happened to Me!

There's something about almost dying that changes you. At age twenty-three, a violent storm sank my boat a couple miles offshore in Hawaii. I struggled for my life for three hours in turbulent, shark-rich waters. When I was at my most vulnerable, watching my sailboat disappear under the waves, I learned something that not only changed the way I see our one precious life—it changed my relationship with the natural world.

# The Swim that Changed Me

I was studying to get a PhD in marine biology at University of Hawaii, Manoa. Hawaii is an expensive place to live, so I got creative and figured out how to get by—purchase a nine-hundred dollar rusty old sailboat and live on it. So I became the owner of a small twenty-foot long house with sails. I couldn't afford an instructor, so I got the next best thing—*Sailing for Dummies.* Mind you, I knew how bad/embarrassing it looked reading it on the deck of my boat for all the world to see, so I read it either at night or disguised in another book's cover.

I felt like I was a pretty quick learner, and I had many adventures on that sailboat. Some of the more memorable included beautiful and peaceful encounters with tons of marine megafauna—imagine whales breaching close enough to touch. I was living the dream...until I wasn't.

One morning, my friend asked if we could go sailing on the open ocean. She knew nothing about sailing, and I'd only had the boat for a few months. I was woefully unprepared (*Sailing for Dummies*, ahem), but that didn't stop me from saying yes. I had gained some confidence on the water, and we naively thought it would be a fun adventure to learn the ropes together.

We took off that morning in strong winds and what seemed like really big waves for the generally calm bay we were in. What I didn't realize is that we were sailing into the storm of the decade—and I hadn't even bothered to check the weather!

As we exited the relative protection of the bay through the channel that cut between the reefs, the waves were much bigger than I had been expecting. I didn't decide to turn around until I was fully out of the channel. The problem was that the channel had closed out just as we exited. That meant the massive waves were now breaking in the channel. A breaking wave is far trickier to navigate than rolling waves. Essentially, we didn't have a way back!

Looking back toward the island, there was nothing but white foam as far as the eye could see. I didn't know my way back—my navigation skills were weak at this point. I wasn't prepared for reentering a channel like this, but I had to try.

I turned the boat toward home and knew our best chance was going to be using the engine to plow our way back through the waves. I pulled the string to start the engine, only to find the motor was flooded and dead. I'd have to navigate a return home with only my somewhat awkward skills with the sails—and with a person who knew less about sailing than I did.

I tried to sail back into the channel, turning the boat with each wave to hit it head-on. That worked for a few waves. Then, one fateful wave hit us sideways and swept me off the boat. Now, I was two miles offshore in a storm, looking at my boat sailing away as my friend held onto the rigging on the side. I screamed and swam with all my energy, but I couldn't get to the boat.

Neither of us was wearing a life jacket. I felt the full weight of my clothes and was struggling to stay afloat. Among the crashing waves, I caught a glimpse of my friend, feet in the water yet still holding onto the boat.

She was somehow able to climb back on, but now she was on a runaway sailboat, heading toward the fifteen to twenty-foot breaking waves on the sides of the channel.

Then the unthinkable happened. As I floated there, I watched my twenty-foot sailboat, with my friend on the bow, get tossed like a rag doll end over end in the breaking waves. I knew in my gut there was no way anyone could survive that. One second it was there—and in the next, the boat had snapped in two and sunk. Everyone and everything was gone.

I tried to swim toward the boat, now maybe a quarter-mile away, but it didn't take many fifteen-foot waves to realize I was going to drown if I kept going that way. I turned and started swimming back toward the shore. I was a competitive open-water swimmer at that stage of my life, so I felt I could swim the two miles to shore if I had to. So I put my head down, took off the rest of my clothes (minus my boxers, which I tied around my ankle) and started swimming.

Forty-five minutes into my swim, I realized that the buoys that I should have been passing were doing something funny. Mind you, there was a torrential downpour. Salt was stinging my eyes, so it was hard to see the shore, but it struck me that I had been looking at the *same* buoy this whole time!

I hadn't been getting closer to shore, I was being swept out to sea. At that point, I saw there was only one buoy left. It was my last chance. If I didn't make it to that buoy, I was a dead man. I would be swept out to sea to drown in a storm in the middle of the ocean. Not good.

I could see it. It was right there, but it took another twenty minutes of swimming as hard as I possibly could to get to that massive twenty-foot beast of a marker. Somehow, I got on it and held on for two hours as the wind and rain pelted my mostly naked body (I had put those boxers back on).

Anything I would have used to contact or signal for help was on the boat. The phone, emergency beacon, whistles, and flares were all useless now. But I knew I was on a navigation marker leading out from the naval base onshore. I thought, *What if they're somehow listening?* So I broke a piece of metal from the navigation buoy and started pounding SOS in Morse code on the channel marker, hoping the Navy station nearby might hear it. (FYI—this is how you do that. Three taps close together, three farther apart, three close. Easy!)

No one heard my SOS signal, but as fate would have it, a buddy of mine who knew I was heading out to sea that day had already hopped in his outrigger canoe to check on us. As he paddled out, he found my friend floating on a life jacket that had emerged from the boat wreckage. They were able to flag down the only other boat on the channel and get to a cell phone to call in the emergency!

Three hours into this ordeal, I was naked, afraid, thinking I had killed another person through my ignorance, and suffering from mild hypothermia. The rain was so heavy I couldn't see the shore, and it was so loud that I doubted myself when I started hearing helicopters and boats.

Once they spotted me, a jet ski with surf-saving boards on the back was deployed by the naval base nearby. I climbed to the top of the buoy, waving and yelling! Thank you, Navy!

The storm was still in full force. Even though they could see me, I still had to find a way to jump to the rescue vessel in one of the gaps between the huge waves that were pounding the buoy. Miraculously, I was able to leap and grab on with enough time to speed away before the next wave clobbered us. Ten minutes of ups and downs that felt like a roller-coaster ride got us inside the bay. It was then that they slowed down to tell me my friend was safe. I felt an overwhelming sense of gratitude and relief. We were alive. We had survived.

After that day, I viewed the world differently. I was in awe of its power—not as an adversary, but knowing I am a part of this thing we call nature. It was an awakening to mortality for a starry-eyed kid who lived and breathed a life of longing to return to the wild, and I have carried this feeling with me into a lifetime of adventures ever since.

I learned respect for what I cannot control, how to weigh and minimize risk in the places I love most (the great outdoors), how to prepare for the unknown, to become "Captain Safety" for myself and others...and I definitely learned to check the weather!

# Life After the Wreck

After the wreck, I didn't slow down. I continued to accrue enough adventures to fill many lifetimes. I got a few science degrees, went to film school, met the amazing woman who became my partner in life and filmmaking (Haley), and we started our family. We've been around the world filming wildlife in virtually every environment, from alpine peaks and rainforest canopies to hidden caves, African savannah, the deep sea (in a homemade submarine), and even the Chernobyl exclusion zone. You can see some of our work on Science Channel, Discovery, and Animal Planet, and you can find most of my short-form science stories on my YouTube channels, *StoneAgeMan* and *Untamed Science*.

Through this work, I have had the absolute pleasure of working alongside biologists who are at the top of their field—who know their study animals and plants better than anyone in the world.

I am forever thankful for this gift of knowledge—and the trust they put in me to tell the world the story of their life's work.

This line of work also brings with it a wealth of stories about plant and animal encounters that did not go well, and we can learn from them. Fortunately for you, I've almost died a few times and my life seems to be riddled with friends and colleagues who have survived the craziest of circumstances with animals in the wild. In researching the survival stories you will read in this book, I didn't have to go far to find many of them. My roommate in grad school survived a grizzly attack and has a scar across his nose to prove it, and an ex-girlfriend now sports a handful of crocodile tooth scars across her chest. I have a buddy who lost an arm and a leg to a bull shark. And the list goes on.

All of these events are extremely rare, yet here I am with a deep trove of stories. At this point, you may be thinking that the takeaway of this book is that being a close friend of mine would be a danger to your health and safety, but I truly hope these experiences and the biology that applies to them will help you see the complex wonder of the natural world and encourage you to explore your own relationship with it.

This book outlines what I wish I had known as an eighteen-year-old kid who set off eagerly into the wild and ended up in too many close calls. You'll find useful tidbits about animals, plants, and fungi to help you avoid dangerous situations.

As you go through this guidebook, I hope it bolsters your enthusiasm for wildlife and nature. To understand each organism, I've combined its basic biology and behavior with known human encounters to give you a guide to living harmoniously with each. I hope any healthy fear is tempered by fascination as you realize your place in nature. The suggestions in this book have helped others in the past, and they just might help you, too.

In other words, I want you to be prepared *and* know that nature is *not out to get you*!

# Wildlife in Media

The movie poster for *Jaws* depicts a girl swimming at the surface of the ocean, with a great white shark lurking below. Talk about a terrible image to take with you every time you set foot in the water!

As a kid, it was forever burned into my mind. Even in the pool, I imagined sharks coming from the vents! I had a recurring nightmare about it. Of course, I eventually learned that *Jaws* was a fictional story. I was told a counter-story—sharks don't eat people.

Now a marine biologist, I still want to tell myself that sharks don't eat people, but the fact of the matter is that...well, sometimes they do. But it doesn't mean we all have to be helpless floating meatballs.

If you know a little bit about the behavior of many of the potentially dangerous things that live in our world, maybe you'll be less scared of exploring on your own. Maybe you'll be safer. Maybe that will make you the master of your domain. Who knows! Maybe your knowledge will grow into an admiration and love that leads to protecting the wild places that harbor those amazing creatures.

# Here Is What This Book Isn't

This isn't a book about how scary and terrifying all these animals are. That does nothing but scare you with the sensational. I also won't take the opposite approach and say that we humans are evildoers in every wildlife incident. It's not about sharks being victims. It isn't a book suggesting crocodiles might be harmless and misunderstood.

Instead, let's first view nature in a very pragmatic way. What are the ways we humans can get into trouble? What are the lessons we can learn from tragic mistakes of the past? What does science say about the behaviors in question? And how can you apply this knowledge so you can feel confident in our wild world?

I hope what you learn here helps clear the way to turning your fears into a love affair with what some would consider the scary part of nature. The scary can give way to awe for exactly what these creatures are—even if what they are is giant man-eaters.

Armed with a new perspective based on science and real-life examples, I bet you will look at animal encounters in a new light. When you watch movies, you might find yourself looking at scenes with a more discerning eye. Think of *Jaws* again, where the marine biologist appears to get eaten by the sensationalized shark villain. Then, contrast that with the modern #Instamodels and shark activists who swim alongside these massive sharks, hoping to make you think they're only gentle giants. The truth is not one or the other. It is in the middle. You can take these facts, make up your own mind, and judge your own risk.

# Here Is What This Book Is

This book is designed as a straightforward guidebook—a *"What if?"* book for encountering wildlife, with a mix of true stories and relevant biology. I'll walk you through many animals that have the potential to kill you, with a heavy emphasis on how to avoid an encounter in the first place. The sections on deadly plants and fungi could fill entire guides on their own, but I'll take you through the basics of each and best practices for staying safe when encountering them.

The last section gives the basics of outdoor survival. This includes knots, knives, fire-starting, and shelter-building. It's often these basics that (with a little practice and know-how) can really save your life.

You can find even more outdoor survival resources and videos through my YouTube channels and via StoneAgeMan.com and UntamedScience.com.

# Stay Cool

Okay. You're about to read an entire book about wild animals and cool plants, and that's exciting. Your brain is going to get filled up with so many neat biological/behavioral facts and ways you might handle dangerous situations in the wild! So just make sure you keep your cool—and for heaven's sake *do NOT get the idea that you should go out and try to interact with wild animals*. You'll clearly see that avoiding danger in the first place is always the best. I know there is a publisher's disclaimer at the front of this book, but I want to reiterate that reading this book will not make you superhuman or totally in control of any situation in the wild. This compilation of information has helped others, and I hope it helps you. Be smart and stay cool, folks.

# A Good Mix

At my core, I'm a storyteller. I like to keep things a little light and cheeky while sharing all these true stories and fascinating things about animals. I'd never write that rhesus monkeys are "famously cantankerous little brats" in a scientific paper because that's anthropomorphic and decidedly unscientific— but if I were describing observations about them in a casual conversation, I might. Simply put, we're writing to you like we'd talk to you. You'll get a good mix of well-researched science and a personal, frank take on each species.

# PART I:

# Wildlife
# Survival Basics

# Which Animals Made the List

## The Big Picture

There are various wildlife species that have been known to kill humans—insects, reptiles, mammals, plants, and mushrooms. But that doesn't mean you should be scared of them. Almost all of them would rather have nothing to do with you. In fact, many of the "attacks" that I list here are defensive in nature—a way to get you out of their space or keep you from eating them. Only a few fall into the category of "man-eaters"—essentially predators that would have humans on the menu if given the opportunity. It's important to note that humans are not an essential or main prey for man-eaters.

This list is also not exhaustive. If I individually described all of the world's top killers, this book would mostly be about parasites, mosquitoes, and humans. Dangers from humans could fill many a psychology textbook and, although parasites are fascinating, I thought it might be more helpful to learn how to avoid getting killed by a bear or a wolf than to learn about avoiding death from bowel obstruction via infection by each of the thousands of different roundworms.

For perspective, here is a quick list of some of the biggest known killers across the globe.

- **Mosquitoes** kill an average of 1,000,000 humans per year, mostly by passing pathogens to us.

- **Humans** (for reference) murder an average of 475,000 people per year.

- **Snakes** kill an average of 100,000 people a year.

- **Dogs** kill an average of 25,000 humans per year—mostly from secondary infections of rabies.

- **Tsetse flies** kill an average of 10,000 per year via a parasite that causes African sleeping sickness.

- **Assassin bugs** kill about 10,000 humans per year via a parasite that causes Chagas disease.

- **Freshwater snails** transfer the parasitic worms that cause schistosomiasis, which kills about 10,000 a year.

- **Scorpions** sting and kill an average of 3,250 humans per year with their toxic venom.

- 🔥 **Ascaris roundworms** kill 2,500 humans per year via malnutrition, tissue problems, and bowel obstruction.

- 🔥 **Tapeworms** kill an average of 2,000 humans per year via malnutrition and interference with organ functionality.

- 🔥 **Crocodiles**, by contrast, only kill an average of 1,000 humans per year.

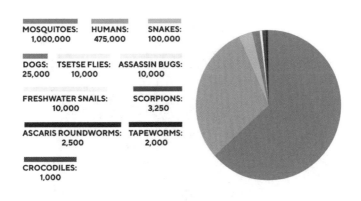

MOSQUITOES:        HUMANS:        SNAKES:
1,000,000          475,000        100,000

DOGS:    TSETSE FLIES:   ASSASSIN BUGS:
25,000   10,000          10,000

FRESHWATER SNAILS:        SCORPIONS:
10,000                   3,250

ASCARIS ROUNDWORMS:   TAPEWORMS:
2,500                 2,000

CROCODILES:
1,000

Sharks, which people love to put up on killer lists, only kill about four people a year! Despite these statistics, I can guarantee you that most people are scared of the unseen sharky threats that live below the waves. Keep that in mind, and let's dive into some wildlife survival tips, should you ever be involved in a rare encounter with some of our planet's unique wildlife.

# Piranha

At sixteen, I bought six piranha to raise in a hundred-gallon freshwater aquarium. In my weird world, that seemed to be the coolest thing I could do as a high schooler. Every time I fed them, I got to see the hunting behavior of these amazing fish. As I put in a goldfish, they'd gradually all get more and more excited. The goldfish always seemed to be oblivious to what was happening around it.

One piranha would start by taking out the tailfin. The next few piranha would take the other fins. After that, the gut. Quickly, at this point, they'd all go in for a bite. It was not a feeding frenzy— it was a precision attack to take out this poor goldfish. Full disclosure, it made me sick the first time. I probably wouldn't do this today simply because I prefer to see them in their natural habitats, but I credit this experience with beginning a lifelong passion for fish, behavior, and, ultimately, awe-inspiring creatures.

If you watch old movies, you may remember scenes of jungle explorers walking through tropical rivers only to get attacked by bloodthirsty killer piranha. There is even a Bond villain who uses a tank of piranha to devour his enemies in seconds.

However, if you are not a villain with dreams of fish murder— you'll be happy to know that piranha are not the bloodthirsty killers the movies make them out to be. Having raised my own, I should know. Watching and caring for them let me see their complex behaviors. They're close to my heart, as far as "dangerous" species go, so I'm excited to give you a closer look at the behavior and biology of the piranha.

And, make no mistake due to my affection for them, piranhas *do* bite—and with razor-sharp teeth. Fortunately, people get bitten only rarely. In this section, you'll get the tools to understand why a bite might happen and what you can do to prevent it.

# The Basics

There are actually many different species of piranha. Depending on the way you classify them, it's between about thirty and sixty species. Most are omnivores, eating a mixture of fruit and meat. Some eat only plants.

They all evolved, and currently thrive, in the tropical waters of South America. In fact, each river basin may have its own unique piranha species. They're not sharp-toothed eating machines that indiscriminately tear apart any living flesh. They are highly adapted to their own river basin and unique food source—and can discern their natural food source from something foreign, like a human. So, what does that mean for you?

Let's get down to brass tacks. If you're on a trip to the Amazon, I'm sure you're going to wonder how dangerous it is to swim in the river. Piranhas are very abundant in most waterways there. If you stick a piece of bloody meat in the water, you're almost certain to pull out a piranha on every cast. But here's the thing— they almost never bite people.

This was also my experience with the piranha in my fish tank. If I had to clean the tank, I'd put my hand in and scrub around. They would cower on the other side of the tank. But when I threw in a piece of meat, they'd jump into action. That's because they're highly adapted to distinguishing between food and foe in their ecosystem. They're very acute predators, but also the prey to other animals like crocodiles, herons, and other, larger fish.

Essentially, they don't want to get killed as much as we don't want to get bitten.

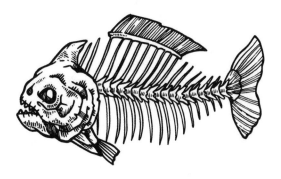

That being said, they have a lot going for them when they do decide to chow down. Piranha have brilliantly adapted teeth and jaws. A piranha's teeth are triangular and sharp to tear through flesh. They lose their teeth on occasion, and new teeth will grow in their place. The jaws are powerful and interlocking. In fact, the black piranha's bite force has been measured at seventy-two pounds per square inch. To put that in perspective, if you were to scale up a piranha to the size of a great white shark, its bite would be almost thirty times stronger than the shark's.

Their teeth are pointy and sharp and can bite through steel wire. They can also easily bite off a finger. This makes it especially tricky when fishing for piranha. Your fleshy thumbs are dangerously close to very sharp teeth every time you need to remove the hook from the mouth.

But what if you're not fishing? What if you just want to go swimming? Well, it turns out piranha are really only dangerous when certain conditions make them dangerous. Let's delve into those conditions and how to avoid them.

# Scenarios to Avoid

**Don't swim in small bodies of water in the Amazonian dry season.** In the Amazon, the rains flood great expanses of rainforest for part of the year—the wet season. The water covers the forest and provides a lot of new habitats and potential food for piranha, like fruit, nuts, small mammals, carrion, and small crustaceans. As the water dries up during the dry season, bodies of water shrink and concentrate large numbers of piranha in smaller areas. As food sources get depleted, they end up very hungry and willing to try new food.

**Don't enter the water with cuts** or open wounds. This is also a safety protocol for being in tropical locations. Bacteria in the water can be even more dangerous than the piranha.

**Don't swim near active fishing** or fish-cleaning activities. Piranha are easy to catch and delicious. It's just common sense to avoid swimming in an area where people are actively trying to get the fish to bite!

**Try not to thrash around in the water.** Piranha are attracted to this type of behavior in the similar way sharks are.

# The Most Dangerous

The **red-bellied piranha** is known as the most dangerous, in part because it's the most abundant and is usually found in groups.

The **black piranha** is the largest and has the most powerful bite. It can devour carcasses quickly, if given the chance.

The largest piranha attack ever recorded was one by neither of these. It was Christmas Day 2013 on the Parana River in Argentina. The temperature was almost a hundred degrees, so bathers were in the water trying to keep cool. That's when a feeding frenzy took place. Over seventy people were bitten by piranha as they scrambled to get out. A seven-year-old girl lost part of a finger. We're still not sure exactly what caused the frenzy. Possibly it was one drop of blood in the water and a bunch of hungry fish—hard to say. In that case, the **spectacled piranha** was to blame.

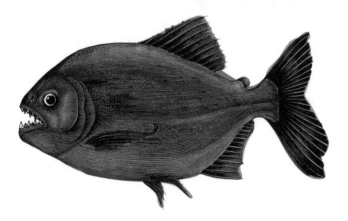

# How to Survive an Attack

Almost always, *attacks* by piranha are simply a single bite. However, a single bite can draw a lot of blood, and more piranha quickly swim in. That means you need to:

- 🔥 **Get out of the water** as quickly as possible if you've been bitten.

- 🔥 **Signal for others** in the area to get out.

- 🔥 **Seek first aid** for your bites as soon as possible.

# The Take-Home

It's important to know that people in the Amazon live in relative peace with piranha on a daily basis. They eat them (again, delicious), swim in the river with them, and use their teeth as powerful cutting instruments when using natural materials for blades. My wife and I relish our visits to the Amazon, and we have noticed that any fear of piranha is something foreigners bring with them from Hollywood portrayals— never from the locals. These sensational stories paint a very biased view of these remarkable and well-adapted fish. We can be safe around piranha and respect their abilities at the same time!

# Venomous Snakes

I vividly remember my brother's first close encounter with copperheads. Our family was sitting around a picnic table at night. One small yellow lamp lit the area. The summer air was hot and humid, even at this time of the night. At some point during our conversation, my dad looked down and saw the copperhead and in a surprisingly calm voice said, "Don't move, there's a copperhead at your feet." For some reason, I was paralyzed, and did nothing at first. After a beat I looked down to see two three-feet long copperheads crawling inches from my bare feet. My brother, on the other hand, jumped back several feet with terror in his eyes. Luckily, this didn't cause a strike toward me or him. I guess we were lucky.

I think we all have a somewhat innate fear of snakes. I know I've never been naturally drawn to them. In fact, it's taken years of watching and handling them to unlearn my initial fear of them. I don't blame my brother for his dislike of snakes. That was a traumatic introduction to them at the age of twelve. Yet, even if you do have a fear of snakes, I'd like to think the safest thing you could do is learn about them so that you can interpret what they're about to do next. Are they ready to strike or are they just curious? What actions can you take to make sure you stay out of danger?

I still stand by the idea that a calm response to the copperhead was the safest approach, but is that always the right approach? Let's dive a bit deeper into these snakes so we can avoid and mitigate negative interactions that may cause harm, or a lifetime of fear.

# The Basics

There are approximately 3,800 species of snakes in the world. Out of all of those, only 375 are venomous.

Yet, for most of us, snakes evoke an almost primal fear. It feels at times like this fear is part of our very DNA. In Genesis, the devil (the personification of evil) is represented in the Garden of Eden as a serpent. In fact, it's hard to come across historical accounts that make snakes out to be kind, loving, and generous. The fear of them is somewhat justified, too. They kill many more people every year than sharks do.

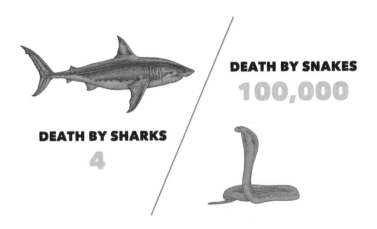

**DEATH BY SNAKES**
100,000

**DEATH BY SHARKS**
4

In fact, the World Health Organization estimates there are as many as five million snake bites a year—half of which cause envenomation (successful injection of poison). Of those, there are on average about 100,000 deaths a year from snake bites. Most of those are in regions where both hospitals and antivenom are unavailable.

Some have hypothesized that the great eyesight we have as humans (only surpassed by predatory hawks), and the fact that our eyes are fully forward-facing, is an evolutionary adaptation for being able to spot snakes in the undergrowth. Surely having this ability would aid in keeping you alive. But are venomous snakes really out to get you?

No. They are not.

The evidence is simple. In spite of the high number of annual deaths from them, venomous snakes don't attempt to eat the humans they envenomate. The toxicity of their venom is an adaptation for two things—immobilizing the prey they eat and providing a defense against predation.

The toxicity of their venom and danger to humans is absolutely not because they are *out to get* humans. Their venom is used to immobilize their prey. Some of the most toxic species have venom that acts quickly so that their prey can't go far and can't fight back before they are consumed. Sea snakes eat fish that can swim swiftly away, so their venom is one of the most toxic and fast-acting. Put simply, venomous snakes have venom that is well-adapted to the prey they eat.

To put it another way, humans are thankfully not on the menu. However, this is of little comfort if someone gets a lethal dose of venom from a self-defensive snake bite. Venoms are chemically complex and highly variable and cause a huge range of deadly and often grotesque consequences in the body. Let's take a look at the basics of snake venom to get a broad view of what we're dealing with.

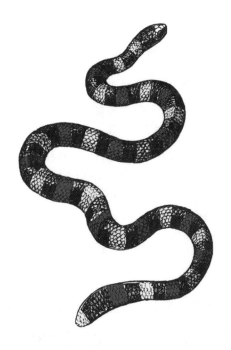

# The Main Types of Venoms

People have a range of reactions to various snake venoms, so it's somewhat hard to pinpoint exactly what happens when someone gets bitten. However, there are five broad categories of venom toxins—hemotoxins, neurotoxins, myotoxins, cytotoxins, and cardiotoxins. Each causes quite different kinds of damage.

**Hemotoxins** destroy red blood cells, causing organ degeneration and general tissue damage. Vipers and pit vipers have this sort of venom.

**Myotoxins and cytotoxins** cause severe tissue damage. If not treated right away, they can cause loss of limbs.

**Cardiotoxins,** as the name implies, affect the heart. They may cause the heart to beat irregularly or stop, causing death. Cobra venom includes a cardiotoxin.

**Neurotoxins:** Cobras, mambas, taipans, and coral snakes contain neurotoxins. These toxins are destructive to nerve tissue and are very dangerous because they can shut down your body's ability to control muscles, like your heart and your diaphragm, which keeps you breathing!

# Is There An Easy Way to Distinguish a Venomous Snake?

The short answer is no, but location can help. In the United States, for instance, we mostly just have to distinguish between venomous vipers and nonvenomous colubrids (the coral snake is the only exception, as it is venomous and not a viper). Because of that, people have been taught to assess head shape and pupil shape.

**Head shape**—Viper heads generally have a very pronounced triangular shape. Of course, there are other snakes, like pythons, water snakes, and other mimics with triangularly shaped heads, so make sure this isn't your only point of diagnosis.

**Pupils**—Vipers are known for their cat-like pupils. They are elliptical and look very different from the round pupils of most snakes. Then again, if you're close enough to distinguish the pupil shape, you're too close.

The real problem is that **not all venomous snakes are vipers**. In Australia, for example, the most venomous snakes belong to a group of snakes called elapids. Cobras, mambas, king browns, and taipans belong to this family. They don't have elliptical pupils or triangular head shapes. Sea snakes are elapids too, and they're extremely toxic. Finally, some colubrids are also venomous. All this is to say that it's not extremely wise to trust general rules until you know a bit more about the snakes you're dealing with in your area.

The best thing you can do, if you live in areas with venomous snakes, is to learn as much as you can about what you might encounter and, to avoid particular situations that might put you at greater risk of getting bit by venomous snakes.

# Scenarios to Avoid

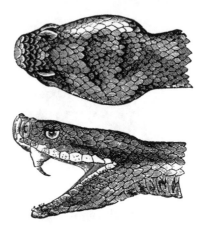

There are definitely certain situations that put you at more risk of getting bitten by a snake. Here are a few.

1.  **Don't stick your hand into holes** without knowing what's inside. Snakes love to find homes in small crevices and will attack if they feel threatened.

2.  **Avoid walking with bare feet** through thick brush without being able to see where you're stepping. The simple solution to this is to wear some sort of boot with thick rubber or leather.

3.  **Snake-proof your property.** Okay, technically you can't ever snake-proof your property, but most people don't want to have a venomous snake near their home, especially if they have young children or pets. A simple way to minimize your chances of an encounter is to keep away mice and rodents, which the snakes prey on. That might mean keeping chicken or bird feed in closed containers. It also means sealing the house properly, with window screens and sealed doors. This will help make

sure you can live in harmony with these creatures without fear of them entering the house.

4. **Don't provoke the snakes.** Many bites happen when people are trying to handle or kill a snake. While I understand the mentality, you should be aware that this may be the most dangerous moment. They can move quicker than you think!

5. **Don't handle a dead snake.** Believe it or not, many people are bitten by dead or decapitated snakes each year.

# The Most Dangerous Snakes

A few years ago, I made a video titled "The Most Dangerous Snakes in the World." It got a lot of criticism because how someone determines the level of danger is a bit subjective. Is it the toxicity of the venom, the amount of venom they inject, fang length, how often they encounter humans, the general demeanor of the snake, or is it some combination of all these aspects? Truth be told, the rankings don't apply well to real life. You might even say the most dangerous snake is the one that just bit you!

Let's take a look at some of the most notable dangerous snakes and why they are in this category.

The **inland taipan** is arguably the most toxic, yet they almost never encounter humans in the wild. In fact, only keepers of captive inland taipans have ever been bitten.

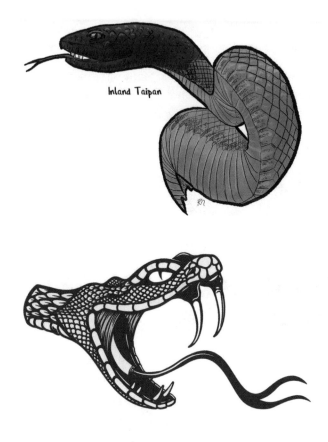

Inland Taipan

**Russell's viper** and **saw-scaled vipers** in Asia and India are responsible for more deaths and are very defensive and difficult to see due to excellent camouflage.

In the US, the **eastern diamondback** is a massive snake that has the potential to inject tremendous amounts of venom.

The **black mamba** and the **king cobra** may be the two most feared snakes for a combination of defensiveness, size, and venom toxicity. Mambas in particular are known for moving really fast.

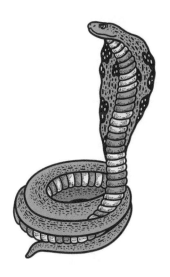

# How to Survive a Venomous Snake Bite

If you're bitten by what you think is a venomous snake, you can survive. Unfortunately, because snake venom varies tremendously, there are some variations as to best practices. Australian snakes, for instance, are often highly neurotoxic and hemotoxic and present unique challenges. However, all venomous snake bites require immediate action. So here are some general steps you can take, should you get bitten.

1. **Get safely away from the snake.** As in any first aid situation, your first task is to make sure you're currently safe and won't get bitten again. Then you can settle down to think.

2. **Stay calm and still.** This may be the hardest part, but if you run and panic, the toxins will quickly travel through your blood to the rest of the body. You don't want that. While you're at it, remove your rings and bracelets (in case of swelling).

3. **Make a plan to get medical attention immediately**. Make a call—get a friend. Do what you need to do to get to the hospital, but make sure the plan isn't driving yourself there. Remember, you may be intoxicated with a cocktail of potent venom! Many doctors use the expression "Time is tissue" when talking about envenomations. The quicker you get treatment, the better chance you have of literally saving your own skin or life!

4. **Mark the bite.** If you have a pen handy, mark the bite site and write the time it happened on yourself. As the redness expands from the bite, you can draw lines around

it on your skin and add the time. This will help the doctors even if you fall unconscious.

5. **Before you go out, always know the local best practices.** In Australia, wrapping and immobilizing the appendage could save your life. The same goes for coral snakes. That's because a compression bandage you wrap on the arm or leg to prevent the spread of the toxin via your lymphatic system will help slow the effects. However, with most rattlesnake bites, if you wrapped the appendage, it would increase the concentration of the venom, which damages local tissue. You don't want that. That's why it's so important to know about the snakes near you and get to the hospital ASAP.

# What Not to Do

1.  **Don't run** or otherwise panic.

2.  **Don't drive yourself** to the hospital. It's likely you could lose consciousness and endanger others.

3.  **Don't cut yourself** or attempt to suck out the venom.

4.  **Don't chase down the snake** in an attempt to bring it to the hospital.

5.  **Don't wash the wound.** This will interfere with the doctor's efforts to figure out what bit you.

6.  **Don't ice it.** This won't help and could damage the tissue.

7.  **Don't put a tourniquet** on a bitten arm or leg. This could lead to even bigger problems.

# The Take-Home

There is a reason we have an almost innate fear of snakes. However, that doesn't mean we need to be paralyzed in fear because of them. In fact, if we only understand a bit about their ecology and behaviors, my hope is that it'll turn into a lifetime of fascination with these magnificent, yet potentially deadly, creatures.

# Reticulated Pythons

## The Basics

The reticulated python is one of the few snakes in the world that can lay claim to being a man-eater. I don't say that just because it has a certain ring to it. There is a huge difference between a man-killer and a **man-eater.** Rhinos can kill humans, but they don't eat them. Plenty of venomous snakes also kill people, and none of them actually eat the humans they kill.

We're talking about a snake that can grow large enough to not only kill a person, but possibly stick around to literally swallow them whole. That's a scary thought!

**Burmese pythons**, **anacondas,** and **rock pythons** are other constrictors that are also potential man-eaters, given their size. Luckily, we've only had a single recent documentation of a reticulated python eating a fully-grown man, so let's concentrate on them.

# Which Snake Is the Biggest?

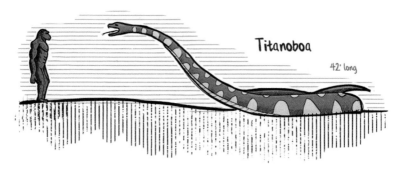

Titanoboa

42' long

How do we measure the biggest snake? The reticulated python is not the longest snake to have ever lived—the extinct *Titanoboa* currently takes that trophy at over forty-two feet long. It's not the heaviest, either—the anaconda claims that title at over five hundred pounds. The reticulated python does, however, hold the record for the world's longest snake living today. Biologists tend to agree that this snake could reach lengths of around thirty feet. However, no snake has been officially measured at that length, and large specimens of these species are becoming increasingly rare due to urbanization and illegal poaching for the pet trade.

*Guinness World Records* lists the largest officially measured living snake as a reticulated python named Medusa—25 feet, 2 inches (in 2011). Oddly, it also lists the largest one ever caught: 32.75 feet in Celebes, Indonesia in 1902, even though many scientists are skeptical of this historical report and think the longest ever may be a bit smaller.

# Reticulated Pythons Can Eat an Adult Human

Everyone always thinks constrictors like the reticulated python kill through suffocation. That is simply not true.

I hosted an Animal Planet show where I investigated the python that swallowed a young man named Akbar on the island of Sulawesi. In the show, I worked with physiologists who studied the power of these snakes. We were able to test a massive Sulawesi reticulated python in a lab setting. By placing pressure sensors inside its next meal (a large pig), we could see that the suffocation myth was busted.

When you crunch the numbers, the limiting factor is the flow of blood to the brain, not how long you can survive without breathing. If these snakes cut off blood supply quickly, the prey die much faster. It's a bit like putting a giant tourniquet on your whole body.

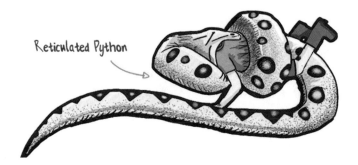

Reticulated Python

The best evidence we have of these snakes being able to eat people is cell phone footage from Sulawesi that shows a twenty-three foot reticulated python with the body of a twenty-five-year-old farmer named Akbar inside.

Now consider the fact that, at twenty-three feet, these snakes can be man-eaters and they can get upwards of thirty feet long. Given that large constrictors like this have been living with humans for thousands of years, it means the largest of these snakes probably *could* have it out for us. If nothing else, if we're within the size range of prey they eat, we could be on the menu. From our perspective, it's an age-old cat-and-mouse game, whose predatory danger has likely been passed down through generations of legends.

The big question for us to consider today is: are these snakes a problem we should worry about?

The short answer is no, unless you live in the jungles of southeast Asia. The long answer is that you shouldn't dismiss these snakes as harmless. They've had us on the menu for a while now. This is even more important to remember if you happen to have one as a pet.

There are plenty of things you can do to avoid an attack and get yourself out, if only you know how. So let's learn how.

# Scenarios to Avoid!

## Walking Blindly in the Underbrush!

The reticulated python gets its name for the "reticulated" or netlike pattern on its back. It has an impressive camouflage, and chances are you won't see it if you're bushwhacking your way through the forest. Reticulated pythons in the wild tend to look a lot like this.

They are sit-and-wait predators that essentially just wait for their prey to come by. And that could be you if you're not careful.

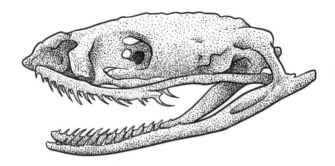

## Don't Get Bitten

Well, duh. Keeping your distance is the best strategy to not get bitten, but much of the time there are no signals to let you know a reticulated python is nearby. They are incredibly stealthy, and it's difficult to find them even if you know there is one nearby. If possible, walk in more open areas where there are limited hiding places. I talk more about prevention and protecting yourself in an attack below, but let's take note why a bite from a reticulated python is particularly gnarly.

Reticulated pythons have eighty dagger-like, backward-facing teeth, organized in six rows. The backward-facing part is key— the teeth are designed to not let you go without taking your flesh right with it. The teeth force the bite, or entire small animal prey, to move in only one direction—further into the python's mouth. Even small pythons can cause nerve damage in your hand via the physical damage from the bite. That means you should not rip the snake's mouth off as it is biting. That could cause a huge laceration. The snake has to choose to let go if there's hope of keeping the chunk it has bitten intact.

## Don't Let It Wrap You Up

Getting bitten is only the beginning. The real danger comes from the constricting power of these snakes. In less than a second from the bite, the python will try to get its first coils around you in an instinctual attack pattern. It twists and spins, disorienting you until it has you locked up completely. Knowing that this is an attack strategy, it is important to work hard and fight like heck (with whatever you've got) from the beginning to keep those coils off. You need to try and uncoil each coil it wraps around you. If it gets too many coils around you, it's next to impossible to free yourself.

# Don't Wander Alone

While having a buddy is always a good thing in the wild, it's particularly important with constrictors. If you have a friend nearby, they can pull the snake coils off or beat the snake until it releases you from its grip and bite. Without a friend nearby, you're in much greater danger. You'll have to resort to other methods of freeing yourself.

# Carry a Stick or Blade

Truth be told, no animal likes to get hurt. Pythons aren't covered in plate armor, so if you do get attacked, a sharp object is going to help you get free, possibly causing the python to open its mouth and let go.

# Let's Recap

Walk in areas that limit the hiding places for a snake.

Don't walk around in heavy brush at night.

Don't wander alone into the bush in reticulated python country.

Don't let your kids or pets wander around alone in python country, as they're easier prey.

Avoid picking up a large constrictor like this by yourself. Even if you do pick it up safely, they have a tendency to wrap up prey quickly—and it's really hard to get out. For perspective, handlers generally go with the *one person per meter* rule when dealing with large pythons (but don't go picking one up yourself without an experienced person nearby).

# How to Survive

Besides trying not to be in the wrong place at the wrong time, there are some things that will get you out of a sticky situation, should you get wrapped up.

Let's just assume here that you've been attacked and the snake is starting to wrap you up.

1. **Don't let it wrap you up.** Keep your hands and arms free. Try to get the coils off quickly.

2. **Control the head.** If you have a friend with you, have them grab the head so you can start unwrapping coils.

3. If it's just you, I guess **it's war now**. Do whatever you need to get free. Just know that, the more you struggle, the tighter it squeezes—it's instinct.

4. **If you have a knife or sharp stick, get it out fast**. Having it on a lanyard on your wrist or neck will help prevent you from dropping it.

5. If you happen to have **mouthwash or alcohol** in your shirt pocket, you could splash it on the snake's face and mouth. They hate that.

# The Take-Home

Pythons, anacondas, and other large constrictor snakes have been evolving with us for millennia. These days, most of them don't get big enough to eat an adult, but that doesn't mean we should be complacent around them.

Let us also not forget that pythons have tremendous value to the habitats they live in and for humans. For instance, they keep rat populations down, which otherwise could spread fleas and disease. Those rats might also eat stored grain, which is a real problem in developing countries. Maybe it's better to think of a python around the house as a gift.

While they're somewhat dangerous when they're big, we can actually live in harmony with them, if only we take a few precautions when we're in their habitats!

# Electric Eels

In March of 1800, the famous European naturalist Alexander von Humboldt decided he wanted some electric eels to bring home to Europe. But he faced a dilemma—how was he to get them without electrocuting himself?

He executed a plan based on suggestions from the locals that the horses could *de-shock* them. So, they sent a group of thirty horses into a muddy pond of electric eels to flush them out. The assumption was that, after they'd delivered their shocks, they could be safely picked up. The theory actually worked, although the sacrifice for this endeavor was two horses—probably from exhaustion and drowning rather than electrocution.

For centuries, there was some doubt as to the accuracy of this story. Now we know it could be true.

# The Basics

Electric eels aren't eels at all. They're a type of electric knifefish that live in murky backwaters of the Amazon. They use their electricity to both detect and electrocute their prey. They also have the ability to incapacitate would-be predators with their powerful voltage.

A single large electric eel can produce 860 volts. For reference, that's seven times the voltage coming out of a typical US power outlet. It's enough to shock a human such that they wouldn't be able to swim to safety and potentially cause death by drowning. If the eel delivers more than one shock or more eels are around, it could stop your heart.

The shock is produced by electric organs that basically run the entire length of its body. Large electric eels can be eight feet long and weigh forty-four pounds.

To understand the danger, however, you have to understand the physics of the shock. Just placing your hand in the water next to an electric eel won't necessarily shock you that much. The electricity dissipates around you in the water. But if the eel either is pulled out of the water or leaps out of the water through aggression, the path the electricity takes is through your body. The shock is worse and potentially very dangerous.

Documented cases of human deaths are rare, although there is always the possibility that it could happen. Most of the "documented" cases of death are questionable secondhand stories. There are stories involving fishermen getting shocked, though, and this should still be enough to make you think twice about interacting directly with electric eels.

# Scenarios to Avoid

**Do not go fishing for electric eels by yourself.** Yes, believe it or not, this is a thing.

**Don't wade through water where electric eels are present without a buddy.** And, while this might again seem obvious, this is how fishermen often fish for electric eels.

**Don't pick up an electric eel barehanded.** That's just asking for a shock.

# The Most Dangerous Electric Fish

As it turns out, of the 350 electric fish, only a dozen are *strongly* electric. Of those, the **electric catfish** (which can emit 300 volts), the **electric ray** (220 volts), and the **electric eel** (860 volts) are some of the most powerful.

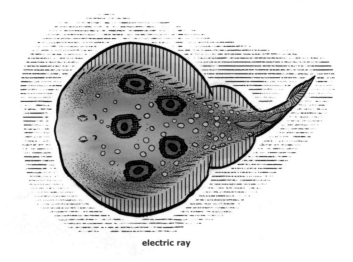

**electric ray**

**electric catfish**

The most dangerous of the electric fish, though, is the electric eel. In 2019, scientists determined that there are probably three distinct species that inhabit different locations on the South American continent.

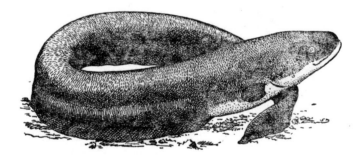

## How to Survive a Shock

The best advice is to not get shocked in the first place. So here are a few more things to think about.

- **Never unhook** an electric eel from your fishing line with your bare hands.

- **Electric-shielding rubber gloves and boots** could prevent a shock if you need to handle one. That should protect you from the voltage.

◐ **Don't drown.** This is where your buddy comes in. If you do get shocked, it usually isn't enough to kill you if you can get out of the water. Drowning is the most common cause of death from eel shocks.

◐ **A buddy can revive you.** If the shock does stop your heart, CPR may be your best bet. If your buddy happens to have lifesaving equipment, like a defibrillator, they could potentially start your heart again.

It's unlikely that you'd just stumble across an electric eel unless you were fishing, so it's nice to know they're not out to get you.

**Fun Fact**

Electric eels are fish that can actually breathe air. They only get around 20 percent of their oxygen from the water, so they surface every ten to fifteen minutes to take in a gulp of air. And if you look inside an electric eel's mouth, you'll find pink folds of tissue that are essentially their lungs!

# Sharks

On our honeymoon in Kona, Hawaii, Haley decided to take me for a fun snorkel in the ocean. The waters were clear, and it was amazing fun to see the fish swimming around. At some point, we looked up to see three kids scrambling out of the water onto the reef with the fear of God in their eyes. They started yelling at us. Two were waving their arms, and one was putting his hand on his head signaling a shark fin.

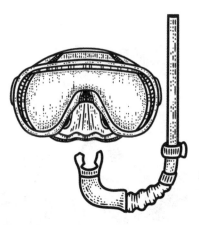

I knew that sign. I thought, *If this is how I go, I'm going to go fighting.* We locked arms back-to-back, so we could keep watch in all directions, and headed for shore. I'm sure it looked humorous—or scary. I don't know. We were scared.

We didn't see it at the time, but apparently there was a massive tiger shark circling us in the bay, staying just out of our vision. I definitely paid more attention while snorkeling after that.

Sometimes I wish my initial view of sharks hadn't been shaped entirely by movies and TV. Mainstream media has been fixated on portraying the dangerous side of sharks since even before *Jaws* came out in the 1970s. But that's not the whole story. Not all sharks are dangerous. It is, however, important to note the evolution of shark behavior and see how it relates to why people may be attacked. For me, this makes

them a bit less scary, and it gives you tools to take with you when you set foot in the ocean.

# The Basics

We should probably stop for a second and remember that "shark" is a name describing over five hundred species. All of them have teeth, but only a few are known to bite, let alone pose any danger to humans. I say this so that you won't fall into the trap of making generalizations about this broad category of cartilaginous fishes.

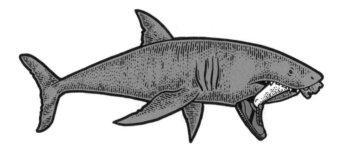

But the fact still remains: they have a lot of teeth, and sometimes they bite people. So what do we need to know to keep these random acts from happening to us?

# Why Do Sharks Bite Humans?

"We're not on the menu for sharks!" Have you ever heard people say that? I have. As a marine biologist, I tell myself that every time I get in the water. Sometimes I repeat it over and over as I swim in murky water. I think it helps. I also told that to the open-ocean swim team I coached for two years. Unfortunately, after I left that club, a shark attack occurred on a nearby beach. I wonder what the coach told them after that incident.

The point is, while it's generally true that sharks don't have us on the menu, they could. Just as, while we don't normally eat cockroaches, we could. Probably not a perfect analogy, but you get the point. We're looking at exceptions.

Put yourself into the role of a shark for a thought experiment here. You have a shark brain—which is very different from human's, so you're roaming the ocean with a skill set that's highly tuned to keep you alive in the world you evolved in (for many millions of years before humans). Your species' very survival depends on getting enough food to get big enough that you can produce little baby sharks.

Each shark species has become really good at eating a particular set of prey, and their behavior is matched to finding and eating it. If we study their feeding and hunting behavior, we can reverse-engineer our survival scenarios for each type of shark. Let's get to it with some general advice.

# Scenarios to Avoid

This might seem obvious, but you're going to want to avoid any situation that makes you either look like shark food, smell like shark food, or sound like shark food, and to avoid being in the water during dinnertime. Let's break it down.

## Avoid Dusk and Dawn

Many of the sharks that bite humans are feeding at dusk or dawn, a time scientists call the crepuscular. It's a tricky time when shark food has a harder time seeing the sharks coming. It's also a great time to catch that last wave of the day, so surfers beware!

## Avoid Murky Waters

Many sharks prey on schools of fish or invertebrates that swim in murky waters near shore. It's easy to mistake a splashing appendage for the movement of a school of fish if they can't see you well.

## Avoid Swimming Near Their Prey

This goes for swimming around boats that are cleaning fish, off fishing piers, and near docks used for fishing. Also, stay away from islands full of seals, but that seems more obvious. You basically want to avoid swimming in areas that the sharks have learned to associate with food.

Before I get to the sharks that are considered the most dangerous, let me quickly point out a shark that is just so unusual and fascinating that I have to tell you about it. My hope is that this helps you see the importance of habitat and the probability of encountering a shark when discussions of "danger" come up.

# The Cookiecutter Shark

I think the cookiecutter shark would be the most feared shark in the sea if only humans bumped into it more often. It lives in the open ocean and feeds at night. That means almost no one runs into one. But if you are in the habit of swimming across the open ocean at night, make sure you pay very close attention here.

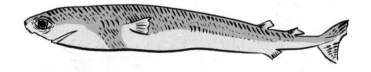

Let me describe this tiny yet ferocious shark for those that have never seen it. It looks like a big cigar, with overly large eyes and a funny-looking cartoon mouth—think of an eel with shark teeth.

What makes these sharks really stand out is their unusual bite. It's a perfect circle! They've found these circular bites taken out of whales, large fish, and even nuclear submarines. Again, for humans, you don't need to worry much unless you're in the open ocean at night and look somewhat like a big fish.

So far, we only have one well-documented bite incident. A swimmer was making an open-ocean swim between islands in Hawaii as the sun set. He swam into a group of bioluminescent squid and felt something bite his chest! Then he felt another bite. He quickly jumped onto the support kayak to see that the holes in his chest were perfect circles—four inches across and almost an inch deep. Classic marks from the cookiecutter shark.

# The Most Dangerous Sharks

Of the more than five hundred shark species on planet earth, only the following four are known to have made more than ten unprovoked, fatal attacks on humans.

# 1. White Sharks

After *Jaws* was released in 1979, white sharks (what people in the film referred to as great whites) took the stage as the most feared sharks, and for good reason. They mainly hunt seals and other large mammals, so humans floating on the surface of the ocean can easily be mistaken for food. Even just a single bite by a large white shark like this can cause death by blood loss. There's no sugar-coating this one. Much like Russian roulette (although with better odds), your best chance of survival is avoidance or luck.

## How Not to Be Shark Food

Don't swim near seals, and pay attention to when white sharks might be in the area. Old studies indicate that these sharks are attracted to bright colors. There is also plenty of anecdotal evidence that white sharks attack seals from below and, given that surfers on boards kind of look like seals, that could put them at greater risk. Unfortunately, it's really hard to do rigorous scientific research on these topics. It's best just to avoid swimming in areas where, and at times when, white sharks appear more frequently. In Cape Cod, for instance, you might not want to swim in the ocean from June to August. In

Monterey Bay, they are most abundant in late summer and early fall.

## 2. Tiger Sharks

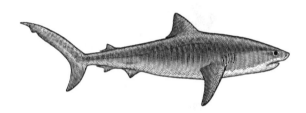

Tiger sharks are big and curious. Sometimes they're referred to as living trash cans with mouths. People have found everything from license plates to parts of tires in their stomachs. This is because they'll bite just about anything to see what it is. It's how they test the edibility of objects in the water.

This means they have been known to approach a swimmer to take a test bite to see what it is. The attack might not be fast, but if you didn't see it coming, you're in trouble.

### How Not to Be Tiger Shark Food

Stay alert. Always look around for the "lazy trash can with teeth." It sounds simple, but you can likely avoid these relatively slow-moving sharks if you remain vigilant during your swim. Then again, they're also routinely seen chasing down and killing dolphins off the west side of Oahu—so they can be quite fast if hunting.

Should a tiger shark approach you, however, there are a few techniques that seem to work. If you have an object, like a camera or stick, with you, you can put that between you and the shark. If it comes closer, a nice punch in the nose often deters them. Or, during approach, you can try the more advanced move of pushing yourself over the shark. Place a hand on its nose, lock your arm and push your way up and over the shark to keep your body away from its shark teeth. These were some of the techniques I was going over in my head as the kids were waving at us from the shore, warning us of that approaching tiger shark.

## 3. Bull Sharks

The movie *Jaws* was actually inspired by a series of real-life fatal attacks in New England in the early nineteenth century. However, it's thought that, because of the location of some of the attacks along estuarine rivers, some of them may actually have been bull shark attacks—not just a rogue white shark.

Bull sharks can be very curious and occasionally aggressive. Add to that the fact that they can swim up rivers hundreds of miles into fresh water, and you have one of the most dangerous sharks.

In fact, bull sharks can actually survive entirely in fresh water. They've been found 2,500 miles up the Amazon. They've also been found up the Mississippi as far north as Illinois and Minnesota. And in Central America's largest lake, Lake Nicaragua, there are resident bull sharks.

## How to Not Be Bull Shark Food

If you're in warm, murky riverine waters, you're in an area that could have a bull shark. The chances of being bitten are low, but it's still advisable to avoid murky waters and to not splash around like a wounded fish. You may just attract a bull shark that comes in to take a test bite.

# 4. Oceanic Whitetips

The oceanic whitetip shark lives in the open ocean. They rarely go anywhere near the shore, and thus are unlikely to encounter most humans. However, it's believed that castaways and victims of shipwrecks may fall victim to these sharks more than any other.

The dangerous thing with oceanic whitetips is that they're very aggressive and curious. They don't have the same fear of approaching a human that other sharks have. So, if you happen to be in the water and see an oceanic whitetip, you should usually get out of the water as quickly as you can.

## How to Not Be Oceanic Whitetip Shark Food

Most oceanic whitetips are in the open ocean, where the water is clear. It should be fairly easy to see an oceanic whitetip coming, so stay alert if you're swimming in the deep blue. When you see one, unless you're with trained professionals, the sighting would be your cue to get out of the water by any means possible.

# The Take-Home

If we start looking like the prey of a shark, it's possible they'll attempt to bite. It's not even that they're confused. They have certain behavioral cues that trigger feeding responses (that's how we talk in behavioral ecology circles). Basically, if you present like shark food, you might become shark food.

Just remember, no shark has ever evolved a taste for humans—we just don't go into the ocean enough.

# Sharks that Have Bitten People

White

Requiem

Wobbegong

Blue

Sand tiger

Hammerhead

Tiger

Bull

Blacktip

Shortfin Mako

Blacktip reef

Grey reef

Oceanic whitetip

Lemon

Bronze whaler

Spinner

Galapagos

Cookiecutter

Blacktip

Nurse

Sevengill

Caribbean reef

Porbeagle

Galapagos

Dusky

Tope

Port Jackson

Guitarfish

Leopard

Mako

# Brown Bears

When I was in grad school in Hawaii, I took a bike trip up the West Coast from Seattle to Alaska, ending in Denali National Park. We camped along the road and saw, on average, a bear every day of the trip. Sometimes we even heard them sniffing around the tent, which was, frankly, really scary.

On a bus tour in Denali (the only way to get into that park), the driver told us over the intercom that they had dropped off a camper a few days before and that there were reports that he had been attacked by a grizzly.

A month later, I asked my new roommate why he had a big cut across his nose. Turns out, he was the camper who survived that grizzly encounter!

He had opened the door to his tent to find three cubs in front. He jumped out quickly to get them away. The mom saw him doing so and charged him. The charge ended in a quick swipe to the nose; then she retreated. Luckily, that's all that happened.

He spent the rest of the night on a cliff looking down at his tent where the mom and cubs had decided to hang out. No doubt, pretty frightening.

# The Basics

Brown bears are the most widespread and diverse of the eight species of bears. They can run at speeds of over thirty miles per hour and have long claws! They can climb trees and swim well. Even small brown bears are in the 300-pound range. The largest ever was a brown bear on Kodiak Island that weighed 1,656 pounds and stood 9.8 feet tall.

Just on size alone, you probably already realize you don't want to mess with a bear. You don't want to get in their way, no matter what they're doing, and you definitely want to know a lot about their behavior so you don't fall victim to a brown bear encounter.

Luckily for you, there are ways to avoid brown bear attacks.

To start, it's important to understand that all bears are really smart. They can solve complex problems and have great memories. That means they'll learn how to interact with humans if given the chance. They'll use these experiences to decide whether you're a threat or if you are potential food.

Secondly, it's important to note that, just as there are good people and the occasional grouchy psychopath, bears are individuals too. Most bears are totally okay with humans in their environment and don't try to get mixed up in human affairs. But, occasionally, a random bear ends up eating someone. Those are the facts. What I'm outlining here is how to avoid confronting any bear and how to look for signs that might indicate trouble.

Finally, let's remember that brown bears are opportunistic omnivores. That means that, while they do consume mammals and fatty fishes, upwards of 90 percent of their diet consists of acorns, nuts, berries, leaves, and roots. This is important information because, for the most part, bears don't view humans as food. Then again, *opportunistic omnivore* means they *could* actually view *you* as food. So, let's walk through how not to get into the wrong situations.

# Step 1: Properly Identify the Bear

The info I'm giving here is specific to brown bears (sometimes also commonly referred to as grizzlies in North America). What you do with a black bear is a bit different. Just take note of the following characteristics.

# Brown vs Black bear

SHORT EARS  SHOULDER HUMP  TALL EARS  NO HUMP  SHORT FACE  LONG FACE

The main reason I point these out is that color is a poor indicator of what bear you're looking at. Black bears can range from pitch-black to white! Brown bears have similar variation.

# Step 2: Understand the Three Main Types of Brown Bears

Just as you'd interpret the danger posed by a teenage human differently from an old man, or a mother pushing a stroller, there are also big differences in bears. Let's go through three specific types of bears you might encounter.

**Yearlings:** These bears have just been separated from their mothers. They're like teenage kids. They don't exactly know what to do yet and are just trying to figure out the world. Curiosity can be their downfall.

**Mothers with cubs:** As the saying goes, don't mess with a mother and her cubs. You will get attacked pretty quick if you get in the way—they're very defensive.

**Lone males**: Lone males generally want nothing to do with you, unless they see you as food. If they attack, you might be in trouble. This is really truer with black bears than grizzlies, but it's worth noting.

# Types of Bear Encounters

Not every encounter is going to be dangerous. Here are a few possible outcomes of meeting a bear.

## Non-Encounter

In this case, you probably won't even know it happened. It hears you and leaves the area. For all intents and purposes, this is ideal for both you and the bear. You may find some footprints or bear scat to know a bear was close, but that's about all you'll find. On a few occasions, we've seen bears on remote cameras stepping away from a trail to let humans walk past them before reentering the trail—so polite!

## Peaceful Encounter

If you see the bear, you can communicate with it in a **calm and quiet** voice. Don't run. These situations often end with the bear just walking away.

## Habituated Bear Encounter

Bears are smart. They've gotten used to humans and, while this might be cute at first, it can lead to trouble. Remember, bears have big teeth and claws!

## Defensive Attack Encounter

Most "attacks" are really defensive in nature. They just want to neutralize the threat. Unfortunately, with a brown bear, a strong hit across the face could be enough to kill you. That's why, if it's a brown bear, the recommendation is to **play dead**. Let them know you're not a threat.

## Predatory Bear Encounter

If a bear sees you as prey, you're in trouble. This rarely happens with brown bears. Black bear attacks of this kind are a different story. I'll get to them in the next chapter.

MOTHER NATURE IS NOT TRYING TO KILL YOU

## Scenarios to Avoid

🔥 **Don't get between a mother and her cubs.**

🔥 **Don't anger a bear.** That means shooting it with anything, especially if it wounds the bear.

🔥 **Don't wander alone.**

🔥 **Especially don't wander in bear country when the bears are potentially hungry** or trying to beef up before winter. Late fall, before they hibernate for instance, is a bad time to confront a skinny bear.

🔥 **Don't have food in your tent.** Bears are curious and always looking for food.

# The Most Dangerous

Generally, bears are peaceful. I'll say that a thousand times. Then again, Timothy Treadwell, a.k.a. *Grizzly Man*, said that too and ended up getting eaten by a brown bear in Alaska. So that raises the question, what is the most dangerous brown bear? Here are a few potentially dangerous ones.

🔥 A threatened mama bear with cubs

🔥 A grumpy or mean bear (but how are you going to know?)

🔥 A habituated bear that associates humans with food

🔥 A bear that actually sees you as food

# Facts about Bear Spray

Everyone should carry bear spray in bear country. It's the easiest and most effective way to stay safe. Here are a few things to know:

1.  Bear spray can reach forty feet.

2.  It causes burning and blindness in the eyes and burning on the skin.

3.  Don't spray it on your tent—you may attract a bear. It's only for direct use when a bear is approaching.

4.  You should carry it on a holster on your body or with a carabiner.

5.  Every person in the group should carry one or two.

6.  Practice using it at least once before you go out.

7.  You can spray two or three short blasts per canister.

8.  Bear spray is the equivalent of pepper spray or mace for humans. It contains the same active ingredient oleoresin capsicum, which is derived from peppers. It just has a smaller concentration. Bear spray is also designed to distribute a wide cloud instead of at close contact, like with a human attacker. Point being, carry bear spray

only for bears, and mace (if it's legal in your area) only for safety from other humans.

9. Studies have shown that 98 percent of the times bear spray was used, it was effective. Only minor injuries were sustained in the other 2 percent of those incidents. In contrast, for firearms, gun use was effective only 76 percent of the time. Those aren't great odds.

# How to Survive a Brown Bear Attack

⬧ **Use bear spray**—it is very effective.

⬧ **Travel in groups** of more than two.

⬧ **Do not startle or surprise a bear**.

⬧ **Do not run!** The bear could then see you as prey.

⬧ Communicate in a **calm tone** with the bear.

⬧ **Be calm** yourself.

⬧ **Play dead** if a brown bear does attack. It most likely is a defensive attack.

⬧ **Lie on your belly** with hands behind your head, ideally with a pack on.

⬧ *Note: Do not play dead with a black bear. We'll get to that next.*

**Tip: Stash your food well away from bears in bear country.**

If you're camping in bear country, the idea is to store *all* of your food in a *bear bag* up a tree. Get it at least twelve feet off the ground and tie the rope to another tree. This should minimize a curious bear's ability to get to your stash.

5

5'

10'-12'

# Black Bears

I've seen hundreds of bears. Most of those were black bears. On two separate occasions, I sat still as a statue while a bear sniffed the perimeter of my tent and rummaged around the campsite. In Ely, Minnesota (home to the North American Bear Center), Haley's very first field assignment with our team was to film with researchers and walk among more black bears than they could count. Imagine walking through a crowd very slowly, but instead of people...you're walking past black bears. It was an experience like no other.

Bears are extremely quiet walkers, so there were times when Haley turned to avoid one bear—only to find an eight-hundred-pound bear was trailing right behind her. They are incredible creatures, and the evening was mostly spent watching bears eating nuts and berries and cubs playing like puppies. At one point, they walked into the forest and gazed up to see that the trees were *full* of bears relaxing in the canopy and hanging from branches. It's the kind of special sight that makes the hair stand up on the back of your neck—and you'll never forget that bears climb trees! For the most part, the walk was what I would call a high-intensity calm.

Then, seemingly out of the blue, a male bear started making some heavy breathing noises and charged a member of our team! It was swift and scary, and then the bear changed direction and wandered away. It was a bluff charge, perhaps to show dominance, and it was certainly an adrenaline-shot reminder that anything can happen in a moment. And, for Haley, I'd say it was a heck of a first day!

# The Basics

Black bears are found all across much of the forested regions of the United States and Canada. Because of that, many more people have chance encounters with black bears than any other bear species. And, for the most part, they're only interested in being a bear and eating nuts, berries, and other bear food.

A large male black bear can easily reach 600 pounds, and thus, they're a formidable threat to humans. In fact, the largest black bear ever reached nearly 1,100 pounds. Females are usually half the size of the males.

But let's be clear here, there are tens of thousands of black bears across the country and almost no one ever has a problem with them—until there is a problem. So how are black bears different from the brown bears we discussed in the last chapter?

First, black bear mothers will attack defensively, but it's much less common than with grizzly moms. Most of the time they'll scatter and try to avoid you. Often a black bear mother will climb a tree and then call her cubs to her. This particular call is easy for bear researchers to identify.

However, if a black bear does attack, the chances that it's a predatory attack are much higher. That means, if they attack, you better fight back. Playing dead just won't cut it here.

# Scenarios to Avoid

- 🔥 **Don't get near a downed carcass** or feeding area.

- 🔥 **Don't leave food out** that can attract a bear.

- 🔥 **Don't feed any bear**—it'll end up making that bear a problem bear, which in the end will get it killed.

- 🔥 **Stay away from a mother and cubs**—which is always sound advice.

- 🔥 **Don't have food in your tent** if you're camping.

# The Most Dangerous

While most black bears are harmless, the most problematic bears are:

1.  Black bears that associate humans with food

2.  A hungry black bear that is willing to consider humans as food

3.  A mother defending her cubs

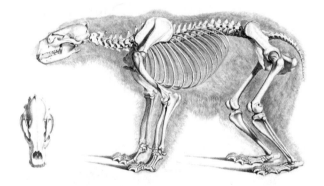

# How to Survive a Black Bear Attack

Most encounters with a black bear will end with the bear running away, but let's walk through a few survival strategies to use if the situation should escalate.

- 🔥 **Stand your ground.**
- 🔥 **If it doesn't notice you, slowly retreat.**

- 🔥 **Never run**—It can trigger an attack.

- 🔥 **Don't climb a tree**—Black bears can climb trees better than any bear. While it's generally not recommended to climb a tree with a brown bear either, a black bear will more likely chase you up into one!

- 🔥 **Don't make eye contact**—They may see it as a threat.

- 🔥 **Use bear spray** to ward off the attack if it gets close.

- 🔥 **Get loud and aggressive** if a black bear approaches. These bears are smart, and you don't want to look like a prey item!

- 🔥 **Don't play dead** with a black bear. If they attack, they're likely attacking because they see you as food—so fight back.

- 🔥 **Sticks and rocks to the face** may be your best bet, if you're in that unfortunate position.

# Polar Bears

## The Basics

Polar bears are the largest and most formidable bear on the
planet. If you're in their country, you're on the menu. This
makes sense if you think about it for even a moment. If you're a
massive predator that has to survive its entire life on a frozen ice
cap, you may have to fend off other predators, but your biggest
concern is going hungry. Polar bears are curious, large, and by
necessity in the environment they live in, aggressive enough to
eat anything.

Most of the year, polar bears look for seals and hunt on the pack ice. When they can't do that, they supplement their diet with bird eggs and occasional berries here or there. For the most part, though, they're meat-eaters.

While some studies suggest that polar bears are going to go completely extinct due to climate change, it doesn't take rocket science to figure out that less ice means fewer polar bears. That's their home. And they are not well-suited to hunting in areas without ice.

More importantly, if you're traveling in polar bear country, and there is anything you take from this chapter, it's to *come prepared*. Unlike most of the other animals in this book, with whom attacks are rare incidents, a polar bear encounter needs to be dealt with quickly, and prevention is the key.

# Scenarios to Avoid

🔥 **Avoid traveling at night** in polar bear country.

🔥 **Don't be drunk and outside**—you'll need your senses with you at all times.

🔥 **Don't attract a bear to your camp** intentionally or unintentionally with food. They are extremely intelligent and will stick around.

🔥 **Don't be out without bear spray or a weapon.**

🔥 **Don't sleep without some form of protection**—inside a vehicle, or with a security fence around you.

# The Most Dangerous

Polar bears, especially hungry males that have washed in from the sea ice, can be a big problem. Even worse are polar bears that have learned human settlements mean food. Remember, polar bears are big and almost always hungry.

# How to Survive an Attack

In the fortunate circumstance that you end up exploring in polar bear country, it is extremely important that, should you see a polar bear, you're prepared. Preparation is your best bet if you're worried about your safety. Bear spray and/or a firearm are key items you need in your kit.

Bear spray is 98 percent effective, so using this is your best bet.

Firearms are harder to use because people don't have much practice shooting something that's running at them. They're only effective 76 percent of the time, as mentioned above.

If you're camping, another great precaution is to use an electric fence to ward off the bear.

Definitely don't act like prey. That means **no running.**

If it doesn't see you, don't do anything.

If it does see you, **make yourself big and act like a threat**. It may be fooled by this. Then again, it may not.

If a polar bear does attack you, playing dead won't help much. An attack means it probably sees you as prey, so playing dead might just make its job easier.

Fighting back may not help much either, because they're incredibly powerful predators with sharp everything. That being said, your best line of defensive attack is to go for the eyes and nose. They're the most sensitive areas and are two things a polar bear needs to continue the attack.

If you survive, you'll be one of the lucky ones! Should you happen to survive a polar bear attack, the silver lining is that you can write an amazing book about it!

**Fun Fact**

Polar bears will actually mate with brown bears in rare instances where their territory ranges overlap. These bears are called grolar bears or pizzly bears. It makes sense that they could interbreed, given that scientists think polar bears evolved from brown bears only about 150,000 years ago.

# Portuguese Man o' War

When I was a kid, my dad went to Florida on vacation and came back with a horrific story of what he described as the most painful sting he's ever encountered.

He was swimming in the shore break when, all of a sudden, a breaking wave engulfed him and brought the tentacles of a jellyfish over his arm, waist, and legs. Immediately the pain rushed through his body. As he fought to get free, he got further tangled up in the jellyfish.

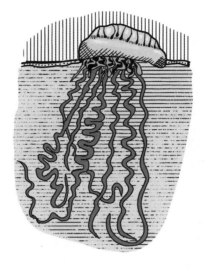

Once on shore, he could look down and pick off the remaining tentacles from his leg. Already there were long red welts on his skin. He felt weak, almost fainted, and had the urge to vomit. "Like my skin was on fire," he explained to me. Peeing on it apparently didn't help (and, as we'll see, this is a myth that actually makes it worse). In total, it took nearly six hours of intense pain for it to start easing up a bit. To this day, he still has a small scar from that incident. The culprit: none other than the Portuguese man o' war.

## The Basics

Possibly laying claim to the best animal name ever, the Portuguese man o' war (a.k.a. man-of-war or blue bottle) isn't actually a single animal at all. It's a colony of variations of the same organism that carry out specialized tasks. One colony is known as a single man o' war. Several floating colonies together are called a legion! And you definitely don't want to find yourself swimming through a legion of them!

Individuals within the colony can't live independently, so you might want to think of them a bit more like a giant group of conjoined twins. Each is unique, but dependent on the others, so all help the colony as a whole.

There are four major types of individuals in the colony (each type is called a zooid). One is specialized to keep it afloat, one for digestion, one for reproduction, and one for hunting. The hunting zooids are the ones we're most concerned with. They're the ones that make up the stinging tentacles!

These colonies can't swim and are thus at the mercy of the currents. That means that, while they may prefer the open ocean, under certain weather conditions, they can start washing up on the shore and getting close to where humans often swim.

All cnidarians have tentacles with stinging cells. They're a group of 11,000 species which include the corals, anemones, hydrozoans, and jellyfish. The Portuguese man o' war makes our list not because it's the deadliest floating cnidarian (the box jelly which I deal with next takes that prize), but because it stings more people each year than any other cnidarian. In fact, tens of thousands of people are stung by them yearly. These encounters result in long, often open wounds on the skin caused by the irritating toxic substances in the tentacles. They leave intense dark purple marks, often in the exact outline of the tentacles that touch the skin. Most remain forever.

Deaths are rare, but I've found at least two confirmed cases— one in Florida and one in Italy. Both seemed to be the result of anaphylactic shock (an intense allergic reaction).

Even if death is rare, you do want to know how to stay away from them, and how to not make the sting of the tentacles any worse than it already is.

# What Causes the "Stings"?

The best way to think about this is that the "hunting" zooids that make up the tentacles contain little spherical capsules that, when triggered, can fire little darts which inject venom. These capsules are called nematocysts, and they're incredibly cool biological venom-injecting structures unique to this animal phylum.

SPINES

This system is designed to quickly capture and incapacitate swimming prey in the ocean. Because of these nematocysts, they're exceedingly powerful hunters.

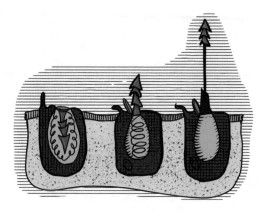

You can trigger a nematocyst to fire its harpoon-like venom-dart through touch, electricity, or a change in salinity.

The reason it's important to know a bit about nematocysts and how they fire is that the treatment and prevention of stings relates to figuring out how to keep them from firing. We'll get to sting prevention, but first let's look at treatment if you get stung.

## Treatment for a Portuguese Man o' War Sting

The treatment is simple. Get the stinging tentacles off your body without causing more of the venom-filled nematocysts to fire. That means...

- 🔥 **Don't rub them off.** The physical rubbing will cause them to sting.

- 🔥 **Don't rinse with fresh water or alcohol.** The change in salinity will also cause unfired nematocysts to release more venom.

- 🔥 **Don't pee on it.** Contrary to popular belief, this is both gross and ineffective. It's pretty likely that your pee will cause the nematocysts to fire.

- 🔥 **Rinse with saltwater or, even better, vinegar.** This will keep the nematocysts from firing.

- 🔥 If you need to pull tentacles off, **pull them off gently** and carefully, trying not to let them touch other parts of your skin.

- 🔥 You may not be able to see some tentacles or barbs that are stuck in your skin. To deal with this, you could cover the area in shaving cream and then **shave the skin**. This will hopefully clean it properly.

- 🔥 For pain, **add heat** around 115°F for forty-five minutes. That'll neutralize the toxins that are in the body already. For reference, that's not quite as hot as a standard heating pad gets. You don't want to burn yourself.

- 🔥 **Hydrocortisone** can also be used for pain relief.

# How Many People Die from Portuguese Man o' Wars?

In 2010, a woman swimming off the coast of Sardinia died from what was believed to be anaphylactic shock from an encounter with a man o' war. Another fatal sting occurred off the Florida Atlantic coast in 1987. Both occurred when a swimmer got tangled up in the tentacles. One can only assume these incidents involved highly susceptible individuals. Then again, we can't know for sure. Deaths are rare. There may be other accounts, but these are the few well-documented cases.

# Scenarios to Avoid

Portuguese man o' wars often get washed up on beaches. Since they don't actively swim, this is a good indication that weather conditions have changed and are blowing them into shallow waters. Avoid swimming without some protective covering if the beach is littered with them. And definitely don't touch the ones that have washed up onto shore.

Most importantly, if you're swimming and do get stung—stop, look around, and try not to get more entangled.

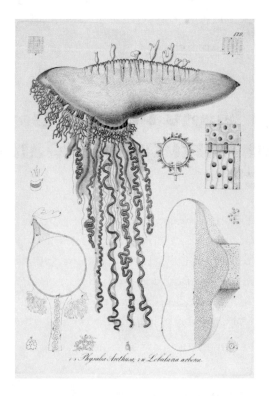

# The Most Dangerous

Technically, there are around twenty species of marine hydrozoans in the family *Physaliidae* that we might call man o' wars. The number is not precisely known, as most are open-ocean species that are not well studied. The two that are most common are the Portuguese man o' war (*Physalia physalis*) and the Pacific man o' war (*Physalia utriculus*). Both are pretty similar and are often called the same thing, so I'm grouping them together here under the same name.

# How to Survive a Portuguese Man o' War Sting

If you do happen to be swimming in the ocean and you feel something sting you, stop. Try to remain calm. You don't want to panic as it could get worse. If it is a man o' war, the tentacles could be up to 165 feet long. Thrashing around will only wrap the tentacles around you.

Now, look around. Let's hope you're not in a legion (a group of man o' wars). What you're trying to do is get out of the water and avoid excessive stings that could cause you to go into anaphylactic shock. Follow the first aid outlined above and seek medical care if things don't get better.

If you see one on the beach or floating by from a safe distance, stop for a second and admire the amazing complexity of this marine colony. You're looking at something that relatively few large marine animals (besides sea turtles and oceanic sunfish) eat, and you're also looking at an animal that produces stinging tentacles that a few other animals use to their advantage. The blue sea slug will feed on man o' war tentacles and incorporate the stinging cells into its own tissue. Other fish, like the shepherd fish (which is partly immune to the venom and lives with the man o' war), take advantage of the protection the stingers give when they swim among them.

Basically, they are cool organisms to see, and they serve important roles in the ecosystem. When you're done admiring them, log the encounter in the memory banks as something to avoid touching next time.

# Box Jellyfish

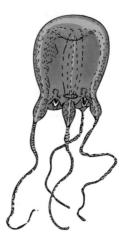

Believe it or not, a tiny little jellyfish takes the title for the most venomous creature on earth! Just getting part of a tentacle on the skin is enough to kill a person within two minutes. We know this deadly creature as the box jellyfish.

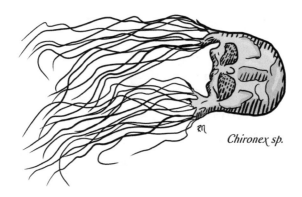

*Chironex sp.*

I hope that got your attention because, if you happen to visit anywhere in tropical Australia or the Indo-Pacific, you need to listen to this! It may save your life.

*Carybdea sp.*

This is one of the few marine animals for which I feel it's okay to start with a paragraph about how quickly it could kill you. Part of the reason for that is that far too many people die from what could be a preventable encounter. You just need to know a bit about these animals to appreciate them, avoid them, and not end up in the hospital, or worse, the grave.

# The Basics

Scientists have currently identified fifty-one species of box jellyfish worldwide. It's estimated that between fifty and a hundred people a year die from encounters, but that estimate may still be low. Many incidents go unreported, since they occur throughout the Indo-Pacific in poor, remote places.

Some box jellyfish are small, about the size of your thumbnail. Others have bells the size of a basketball—with ten feet of tentacles trailing behind them. All have the ability to inflict painful stings, and a few are well-known to quickly kill a human.

Here I'll primarily discuss how to survive Australia's box jellyfish (*Chironex fleckeri*). It is the biggest and arguably the deadliest. It's commonly called the Indo-Pacific box jellyfish or Flecker's box jellyfish.

Unlike other jellyfish, box jellyfish actively swim and hunt for their prey! An adult can swim upwards of four knots in short bursts—that's as fast as you can walk. In addition, they have eyes. They're not exactly like ours, but they do detect rudimentary images and can see in all directions. They can see dark objects better than light objects and will actively avoid them in the water. This is one reason dark clothing is better than light when in box jellyfish waters.

A box jelly has clusters of fifteen tentacles that attach at the four corners of the box-like medusa—that makes a total of sixty tentacles. Each tentacle can be up to ten feet long, and scientists estimate an adult man only needs about six or seven feet of tentacle to touch him to provide a lethal dose of venom. That means a box jellyfish has enough venom to kill nearly sixty humans.

Venom is injected in the same way it is with other cnidarians, such as the Portuguese man o' war that we discussed in the previous chapter. Small cells with nematocysts will fire upon touch or chemical stimulation. In this case, there are hundreds of thousands of nematocysts that fire per sting. These hooked, dart-like syringes dispense the venom into their prey—or our skin. A box jelly is estimated to have about five billion nematocysts!

The venom of a box jellyfish is different from other stingers. It's a complex concoction of compounds, none of which are very well understood. We know it contains a multitude of compounds that, when injected together, work very effectively to immobilize and kill the jellyfish's victims. For humans, it acts in three main ways.

1. It causes skin death. That results in permanent scarring of the skin.

2. It destroys blood vessels.

3. It produces intense muscle spasms that are so severe that muscles of the heart can't relax between contractions, stopping blood flow.

**Symptoms of a box jellyfish sting include:**

⇒ Pain, itching, rash, welts

⇒ Nausea, diarrhea

⇒ Swollen lymph nodes

⇒ Muscle spasms

⇒ Coma

⇒ Heart failure

⇒ Death

*Tripedalia sp.*

Fortunately, there is an antivenom, which many lifeguard stands in box jellyfish territory do carry. Unfortunately, the venom acts so quickly that, if the antivenom is not administered right away, it may be too late.

# What the Venom Does

The venom is a mixture of many things. Each component acts on a different part of the body. One component causes localized pain. Another component travels through veins and arteries straight to the heart. After a sting, the pain comes on quickly and continues to get more intense and spreads throughout the body—ratcheting up the pain with each passing moment.

# Scenarios to Avoid

This general advice applies to all areas of the box jellyfish's range, but is especially important in the warm, murky waters of Australia's northeast coast in summer. This area is home to crocodiles and box jellyfish, so this info is a bit of a two-for-one avoidance strategy.

- **First, always wear protective clothing.** Any kind will do. Lycra suits or even pantyhose will reduce risk while swimming, especially in the summer months.

- **Swim only on patrolled beaches**, preferably in netted swimming areas.

- **Do not run or dive into the water;** walk in slowly.

- **Do not allow children to enter the water without protective clothing**, nor to swim unsupervised during the summer danger season.

- Take the trouble to **be educated in the fundamentals of rescue and resuscitation** from a sting by a box jellyfish.

# The Most Dangerous

The most dangerous of the fifty-one species of box jellyfish is the Australian box jellyfish (*Chironex fleckeri*), which is why I'm highlighting it specifically here. Others (like *Malo kingi* and *Carukia barnesi)* may be called by the common name, Irukandji jellyfish. They're often very small (an inch or less), but they pack enough venom to kill a human. Novelist Robert Drewe described the sting as "a hundred times as potent as that of a cobra and a thousand times stronger than that of a tarantula."

Let's not forget that there are types of box jellyfish all over the world. The Caribbean and Gulf of Mexico, for instance, host a species that is capable of killing a human as well.

# How to Survive a Box Jellyfish Sting

- Immediately **get out of the water**, before you possibly lose the ability to swim and drown.

- **Pick off the tentacle** if it's still on the body. Make sure not to touch it with bare hands—use gloves or utilize a piece of clothing or a towel.

⇒ **Rinse with vinegar** if it's available. Do so generously. While there is still some debate as to whether this is helpful, it's not harmful.

⇒ **Get immediate medical attention.** If antivenom is available, it can be given to counteract the effects of the venom.

⇒ **There are some important things not to do.** Don't pee on the sting or tentacles. Don't rub the area that is stinging. Don't put baking soda on the sting. All of these actions are likely to cause more nematocysts to fire—increasing your dose of venom.

# Killer Bees (Africanized Honeybees)

When I was six years old, I was playing on a playground when a bee decided I was too close to its hive and stung me. It was the worst pain I had ever felt, and the memory of it is still vivid today. But that wasn't a killer bee—just a normal honeybee.

Now imagine getting swarmed, chased, and attacked by thousands of stinging *killer bees*. Potentially, you could go into anaphylactic shock. That pain seems beyond my imagination, as I've still only felt a sting or two at a time—and those are no fun.

Swarms of "killer" bees have been causing very real problems since they escaped from a "science experiment gone wrong" about half a century ago (more on that later). They will chase and sting you to death if you get too close to their hive. Amazingly, this isn't science fiction. It really does happen on occasion. And, if you're unlucky enough to accidentally run into a hive, there's not much more to do other than run as fast as you can in the opposite direction. But if you know a bit about their fascinating biology, you can avoid a potentially life-threatening situation.

# The Basics

These bees should never have existed. It all began with the European honeybee—the bee most associated with honey and beekeepers. If you can believe it, honeybees are actually a domesticated animal. These little buzzing insects have been selectively bred over the ages to be fairly docile honey producers and, more importantly, crop pollinators. Honeybees are responsible for pollinating 30 percent of crops in the US, producing our bounty of fruits and vegetables—the importance of bees to our survival cannot be overstated. In addition, they constitute a 4.5 billion dollar industry in the US alone. But the European honeybee is not used to pollinate crops everywhere in the world. It doesn't fare well in tropical climates—like Brazil.

ESCAPED
IN 1957

In need of a better bee to pollinate crops in warmer climates, a scientist in Brazil crossbred European honeybees with the hardier, but more aggressive, African bees. The hope was that they'd be more adaptable to the heat and humidity. It worked. Then it all went wrong in 1957, when twenty-six swarms escaped quarantine. By 1980, they had covered the South American continent and were rapidly spreading north. By 1990, they had reached the US, and they're still spreading. Here is their predicted final northern range, but there is a possibility this estimate is conservative.

KILLER BEE
POTENTIAL RANGE

# Quick Facts

Killer bees (or Africanized honeybees) don't produce quite as much honey, but they are well-adapted to heat. They are also very good at defending their hives—an aggressive trait we can probably attribute to the African bees.

European honeybees might attack a hive intruder with 10 percent of the colony. Africanized honeybees will attack with nearly the entire hive—and do it within about three seconds of being disturbed. On top of that, they'll keep chasing the intruder for upwards of half a mile from the hive!

Currently, the global death toll from Africanized honeybees is around a thousand people—roughly sixteen a year. Fortunately, as the years go by, the annual number seems to be dropping a bit. This ranks the killer bee higher than shark deaths per year, which is only about four. Thus, these bees are something to be taken seriously!

# How Death Occurs

Death can occur in two main ways—by anaphylaxis and through an overload of venom.

First, I should note, a European honeybee and an Africanized honeybee have the same venom—your body will react the same way if stung by either. So, if you are allergic to any bee, you'll also be allergic to Africanized bees. A serious reaction often includes anaphylactic shock, trouble breathing, and respiratory distress.

The other way Africanized honeybees can kill is by the sheer volume of stings. It has been estimated that over a thousand stings are enough to cause the more serious side effects, including dizziness, nausea, diarrhea, vomiting, increased heart rate, respiratory distress, renal failure, and eventually death.

Stinging is a death sentence for the bee—they are essentially kamikaze defenders. When a bee stings, most of the time it flies away, leaving the stinger, venom sacs, and the bee's insides attached to the victim. It can rarely pull the stinger out without fatal consequences.

VENOM SACK

# Scenarios to Avoid

This one is simple. Avoid disturbing a nest that you can't run away from. For the most part, Africanized honeybees are found in the drier and hotter parts of the US and in Central and South America. There is no sure way to avoid a nest, as they're often tucked away inside a building, a cave opening, or some other crevice. But, if you hear the buzzing of a few bees, be alert. You could have just stumbled upon the hive!

# The Most Dangerous

The most dangerous situation is unknowingly disturbing a hive with no way to escape and having no protective gear covering your body. An example might be climbing a cliff and accidentally disturbing a nest with no easy way to escape.

**The danger is, however, decreasing over time in some places.** We know this because of studies in Puerto Rico, where the bees finally invaded. Studies are showing them to be less aggressive there. While the first theory was that they're interbreeding with less aggressive European honeybees on the island, no one really knows what's happening. Studying the changes in those bees may be the key to dealing with these invasive bees who are here to stay.

# How to Survive an Attack

In general, don't swat at stray bees. The best thing to do is to move away slowly and scan the area for signs of a hive. Swatting a bee close to the hive could trigger the release of pheromones that signal to the rest of the colony that you're an intruder.

If that happens and the entire hive begins to attack, cover your head and run for cover as fast as you can. Get into a vehicle, a building, a tent, or even jump into a river!

Do not stop to try and swat or kill them—that will make things even worse.

If you have access to smoke, use it. When honeybees are alarmed, they emit pheromones that the other bees smell and get alarmed. However, smoke seems to interfere with the bees' ability to smell these compounds and will quickly calm them down for about ten to twenty minutes. But, if that's not an option, your best bet is to get under cover or just keep running.

# Wolves

In 2014, I hosted a documentary investigating the so-called radioactive wolves within the Chernobyl exclusion zone, the fallout zone of the worst nuclear disaster in history. We were looking for wolves in the legendary forests of what is now northern Ukraine. A big reason we were there was the reports of aggressive wolves attacking soldiers inside the zone. Thus, we set out to figure out the mystery and get to the bottom of these "radioactive wolves."

For ten days, we set camera traps and worked with a local wolf biologist to understand their behaviors. At one point, we called the wolves to within a hundred yards of us. The sound of a wolf howling back at you in the radioactive forest of Chernobyl is both thrilling and chilling. It is so much louder than you'd expect, and hearing them all around you is a bit unnerving.

It turned out that the radiation wasn't what was making the wolves more aggressive. Instead, rabies was causing the wolves to attack the soldiers. In fact, while the wolves there did have relatively large amounts of radioactive isotopes in their tissues, the damaging effects of that were much less than the usual hunting pressure from humans. Inside the zone, they're actually doing three times better than in areas outside the zone!

Oddly, I've never really feared wolves. Just about every old fairy tale and legend portrays them as killers. But I also watched Kevin Costner's *Dances with Wolves* (a classic movie about a Civil War soldier who befriends a wolf). Plus, there were no wolves in the woods when I was growing up. I never heard local stories about attacks or even sightings. But today, wolves are returning to our natural landscapes. So what is the truth? Are they to be feared, loved, or both?

# The Basics

If you didn't already know this, dogs are a recent evolutionary offshoot of wolves. So when you talk about wolves, you're talking about the ancestors of modern dogs. With that said, think about your relationship with dogs. Most people know of a sweet dog and potentially also have had some interaction with a mean dog. There are varying degrees of aggression in dogs. Part of being a human today is learning to read their behavior and avoid getting bitten. That's exactly what we're going to do here with their wild cousins, wolves.

Before we start, keep this important framework in mind—dogs are the domesticated versions of wolves. That means, all dogs started a long time ago with wolf genetics. Over time, we selected dogs for different characteristics. Sometimes it was to be good-natured and loyal to us, and other times for a particular color or for hunting aptitude. We've even bred dogs to be more aggressive and better at fighting and attacking. Dogs have significant variation in characteristics. Wolves do as well. Even with gray wolves, which I'll be concentrating on here, there are differences in behavior depending on where they live.

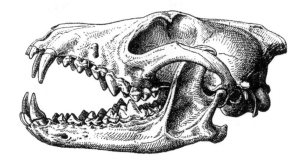

In their natural habitat, wolves survive as predators that hunt in packs. By hunting in a group, they can take down large prey like moose, bison, and musk ox. These are formidable animals, and thus, from a capability standpoint, wolves could easily take down a human. A person going for their morning run would be easy picking for a pack of animals that can take down a moose! The fact that they don't attack humans more often is a testament to how smart they are—and to the fact that humans aren't really on the menu.

Even so, there are countless legends of ferocious wolves, from "Little Red Riding Hood and the Big Bad Wolf" to werewolves. These European legends almost always portray them as the villain. These stories have inculcated in most European and Asian cultures a deep-seated fear of wolves. Yet, it's worth pointing out that these stories didn't exist in Native American cultures in the New World. While you might interpret this fact in different ways, it could be an indicator that the behavior of European and North American wolves is very different.

Many of these European legends stemmed from a very real danger of Eurasian wolves in the recent past. In France, where the best records of this type were kept, there were 7,600 fatal wolf attacks from 1200 to 1920. Even in the last fifty years, when wolves have been mostly eliminated across the world, there were eight fatal attacks in Europe and Russia and two hundred in South Asia.

But let's be clear, before we move on, that you have to take all of the historical data on wolf attacks in context. Dog bites kill an average of 25,000 people a year, mostly from rabies infection. Plus, there are thousands of hikers roaming wolf country in hotspots like Yellowstone and Banff with no attacks to report. States like Minnesota, Wisconsin, Oregon, Washington, and Idaho have had almost no problems between people and wolves. This is important to point out because you shouldn't really be afraid of wolves, at least in the modern world we live in. But should you somehow bump into a wolf pack that's brazen and aggressive, here are some recommendations for what you might do.

# Scenarios to Avoid

**Be cautious if bringing a dog off-leash into wolf country.** If this doesn't make sense right away, think about the conflicts that often occur at dog parks when a dog gets into a tussle with a bigger dog. It's the dog-dog interaction that sometimes leads to the conflict. The same can happen with wolves.

**Avoid hiking and camping alone in areas wolves are known to traverse.** Rangers at stations and campgrounds are good resources to ask for information on wolves in the area before hiking in and setting up camp.

**Don't habituate a wolf to humans**, either by feeding them or letting them get too comfortable around you. This is when conflicts occur—if not for you, then possibly for others. The reason for this is that wolves are smart and quickly learn from humans if given the chance. They may try to outsmart you or treat you like one of the pack. If that does occur, you better hope they treat you like the alpha.

**Stay away from fresh wolf kills**, dens, or rendezvous sites if you happen upon them. Again, park rangers are a great asset for local knowledge so you can minimize your risk of ending up in a risky area.

**Don't let children play away from camp** or alone in wolf country. These canines are large, and a child is easy prey.

# The Most Dangerous

More often than not, wolf "attacks" happen either with wolf-dog hybrids or in facilities where wolves have become habituated to humans. Habituated wolves tend to commit more attacks simply because these aggressive and large animals are used to being in close contact with humans. For perspective, though, while there are only a few wolf-related deaths a decade, about 4.5 million dog bites are reported each year in the US alone, and lead to about thirty to fifty deaths.

The most dangerous wolf, however, is a **rabid wolf**. If wolves contract rabies, they develop what is known as the "furious" phase of rabies to a much higher degree than other animals. Mix that with their size and power, and you get a formidable rabid animal.

Rabid attacks usually occur in the spring and fall—and, for each animal, only during the course of one day. From 1950 to 2002, there were eight fatal rabid wolf attacks in Europe and more than two hundred in southern Asia. Of note, that's also where a lot of the dog-rabies cases originate.

# How to Survive an Attack

If you see a wolf, most of the time it will run away. They want nothing to do with you. Wolves are so stealthy that actually encountering one could be seen as a lucky experience—I've only seen wolves in the woods at random a few times. Of course, if something else is at play and you encounter wolves in the wild that you think are acting predatory in nature, here are some steps you can take to get out of the situation.

1. **Stay calm**. They're smart and, because they're pack animals that test their prey for weakness, they will be testing you.

2. **Don't run.** For goodness' sake, this is the worst thing you can do. Running instantly puts you in a prey category in their minds—and you're not faster than a wolf! If you've ever had a dog bite at your heels, you know this. You can think of it in a similar way for wolves—but with higher stakes.

3. **Let them know you're dominant.** That means you make yourself big and tall. Wave your arms. You should maintain eye contact. We are not a wolf's normal prey, but they're smart. Don't let them learn you're weak.

4. If you do encounter a wolf when you have a dog, bring your dog to your side and leash it immediately. Stand between the wolf and your dog. That often ends the encounter.

# The Take-Home

If you do get to see a wolf, you really are lucky. They've learned how to navigate their environment through trial and error over many millennia. In Eurasia, they have learned, through hundreds of thousands of years living side by side with humans, that we're not ones to be messed with. Wolves instinctively keep their distance. While a few rare aggressive encounters pop up in the news, they're the exception, not the rule.

Now that you know a bit about wolf behavior and have a few key survival strategies up your sleeve, my hope is that you can have a sense of joy in the rare event that you see a wolf from a distance. They are amazing creatures.

# Poison Dart Frogs

It seems odd to me that arguably the most toxic vertebrate isn't anything that is in any way "out to get you." Instead it's a cute, colorful, and passive little amphibian. The **golden poison dart frog** is said to contain enough toxin to kill ten to twenty men just by touching it. That's a pretty amazing feat, given that these frogs aren't much bigger than your thumb!

One conversation I had nearly twenty years ago with a former Army Ranger forever fascinated me with poison dart frogs. He described a training mission with a young recruit who died unexpectedly after getting a simple cut from his own pocketknife. As it turns out, a week earlier he had been messing with one of these poison dart frogs in the jungle—something I can tell you is not good for your karma. The result was a dead frog on the end of his blade. He never cleaned it, and in a terrible twist of fate, he cut himself with the tip of his knife. The toxin entered his skin and caused cardiac arrest within a few minutes.

# Poison Dart Frog Basics

There are more than two hundred species of little frogs that live in the neotropics that are collectively called poison frogs—or more colloquially, poison dart frogs. The latter name came from the fact that indigenous hunters would dip their blow darts in a concoction made of dead frogs to make their blow darts extremely lethal. Truth be told, this isn't true for every species. Only a few have the intense toxicity for that. The most potent one is *Phyllobates terribilis*—the golden poison dart frog.

This frog is bright yellow, and it stands out dramatically in the forest undergrowth. This dramatic coloration is a type of aposematism—advertising with bright colors that they're toxic! In fact, if you see brightly colored frogs, snakes, or insects, this is generally a great indication that they're highly toxic (or potentially mimicking something that's highly toxic). That's why almost every poison dart frog is beautifully colored.

If disturbed, they'll secrete these toxic compounds via glands on their necks and backs. The most toxic compound is batrachotoxin (although they make a host of other toxic alkaloids as well). Just a small amount of it, the equivalent of two grains of table salt, is enough to kill a person. For perspective, this toxin is a thousand times more potent than cyanide.

Batrachotoxin is a toxic cardio- and neuro-steroidal alkaloid. It works by destroying sodium channels—which is essentially how our nerves communicate with each other. This causes paralysis, and since you need your nerves to breathe and to keep your heart beating, it can result in cardiac arrest and respiratory failure. Plus, there is no antidote. Get it in your system, and you're likely dead in a few minutes.

Yet, when living in captivity, they are completely harmless. These frogs could theoretically produce this deadly toxin when they are bred outside their native habitat—that is, if they were given certain supplements or fed a diet similar to their wild one. But that almost never happens. The toxic alkaloids originate in their environment from their unique and not well-studied diet. We still don't know exactly what mystery insect they eat to produce the toxin. Possibly it's a beetle, yet those beetles also accumulate compounds from something else—so the original synthesizer remains unknown.

# Scenarios to Avoid

 If you see any brightly colored frog in the neotropical forests, there is a good chance it's either a poison dart frog or some other poisonous amphibian. Here is what not to do.

- **Don't pick it up**. The stress of handling will cause it to release toxins which will get on your hands and potentially into your skin. Most frogs have some sort of irritant or toxin that they use as a defensive mechanism. Plus, you could potentially harm the frog via lotions or insect repellant on your skin. Remember, many of these frogs are highly endangered.

- 🔥 If you've picked it up, definitely **wash your hands** afterwards.

- 🔥 **Don't touch your eyes, nose, or mouth**. This is how a toxin could enter your body.

- 🔥 Definitely **don't kill it** with a knife and forget to clean the blade. That's how that Army Ranger died. The natives have known this too. There are reports that it remains chemically stable for up to a year on blow darts, which is part of why they're so useful as a hunting tool.

# The Most Dangerous Poison Dart Frogs

 The most dangerous is the golden poison dart frog. It lives in the untamed western Pacific lowland rainforests of Colombia, in one very small region about the size of New York City. It's extremely endangered because of illegal collecting. Fortunately they are somewhat protected by the fact that it's a hot spot for drug smuggling, illegal gold mining, and general civil unrest. That simply means it keeps the average poacher out—let's just hope circumstances don't lead to the extinction of this amazing amphibian.

# How to Survive

These frogs aren't going to attack you—don't worry about that. This is an easy one—just don't mess with them.

If, however, you get a dart in your hip from someone who used the toxin from a poison dart frog—you're in a very different situation. Scientists have found a way to inject certain amino acids found in these frogs into rat muscle to make them immune to the toxin, but that's not something you can do after the toxin starts working in you. **There is no way to counteract the poison** post-hoc, and it acts very quickly. Avoiding the situation is the best thing you can currently do.

I should note that, not only are these frogs *not* out to harm you, but in fact, the toxins from many of the poison dart frogs can save you. There are a number of species in which scientists have used proteins in their toxins to make painkillers fifty to a hundred times stronger than morphine. This is a tremendous breakthrough, as morphine can bring with it a lot of adverse side effects. While I always see saving frogs like this as a moral issue, in this case, it's a clear benefit for us to learn as much as we can about their toxins for our own health.

# Scorpions

Scorpions kill more people a year than almost any animal in this book. In fact, if you exclude mosquitoes and pathogens spread by insects, scorpions are number one. On average 3,500 people a year die from their painful and deadly stings. But they're not doing it because of some ill intent—animal behavior doesn't work that way. They're just being scorpions. Let's get into it.

# The Basics

Scorpions have intrigued us for millennia—and almost always in a way that creeps us out. They've made it into our myths and legends time and time again. In the Bible, they're grouped with snakes as symbols of evil. In ancient Babylon, astronomers saw scorpions in the sky, and Scorpio became one of the twelve zodiac signs. This was surely because scorpions are supreme arachnid hunters in the parts of the world where many of these cultures originated.

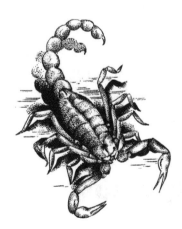

All scorpions are venomous, but generally they're shy creatures and don't intentionally harm humans. Most of the time they sting us because we've stepped on them or put a hand into a glove or shoe that they decided was a great resting spot.

If you find them out and about, it will generally be at night. They're nocturnal predators and use venom to kill their prey.

They then use their digestive fluids to turn those prey items into a meal that can be easily consumed.

But of the 1,400 species of scorpions, only about a dozen are potentially deadly to humans. Those most at risk of a deadly scorpion sting are pets, small children, and those with preexisting health issues. The good news is that, in almost all cases, an antivenom is available if you can get to the doctor quickly enough.

# Scenarios to Avoid

- Don't put on your shoes in the desert at night without checking them. A good way to do this is turn them upside down and bang out any insects. After that, you just have to hope you've gotten them out.

- Babies and small children should be kept off the floor in regions with deadly scorpions. If you're unsure if that's your area, start by asking the locals. The hotter, drier parts of the world are the fullest of scorpions.

- Seal the threshold under your door at night. This keeps them in their habitat and gives you peace of mind.

- Move cribs away from walls and curtains. This is how scorpions usually get into baby beds.

# The Most Dangerous

The most dangerous of all scorpions is the **Indian Red Scorpion**. It often takes shelter near people in rural India. The mechanism of the toxin is unclear, but it's thought to act on the sodium channels that make nerves and muscles work. This can cause heart failure and respiratory paralysis.

The **Arizona Bark Scorpion** is the most venomous North American species. It emits a nerve toxin so potent that it can quickly kill a baby.

**Other notable dangerous scorpions include:**

🔥 Death stalker scorpions

🔥 Arabian fat-tailed scorpions

🔥 Yellow fat-tailed scorpions

🔥 Black spitting thick-tailed scorpions

# How to Survive a Scorpion Sting

You've been stung. Now what?

🔥 If a baby is stung and starts screaming and crying inconsolably, get them to the doctor immediately. One of the telltale signs of the nerve toxin is that it will cause their eyes to roll in their head in an unnatural way.

🔥 Since the venom can impede your ability to breathe, much like a reaction to a bee sting, anaphylactic shock is a possibility. Put victims in a position to promote airflow, preferably on their side.

🔥 Get rid of the scorpion so it doesn't sting someone else.

🔥 Heat can help relieve the pain, and ice cubes help to a lesser degree.

🔥 Get medical attention immediately—antivenom is available for certain species, like bark scorpions, if you can get medical help quickly. If you get the antivenom within an hour or so, you are very likely to pull through.

# Bats

A few years ago, I got special access to look for a long-lost artifact under the holy city of Jerusalem in an abandoned Byzantine church. While that's a story in itself, the one thing we saw a lot of was bats. The entire area was dusty, and bat guano (a.k.a. bat poop) was all over the ground. I've hosted many shows where we're in close contact with bats in caves. They're my least favorite part of the job, but not because of the bat. It's because of the poop.

On this unfortunate expedition under Jerusalem, the producer of the show contracted histoplasmosis from that experience and had to have medical treatment after filming ended. But don't worry, if treated early enough, it's not a terrible disease. He was fully recovered in a few weeks. Thank goodness.

If you think bats are out to get you, then you've probably been watching far too many vampire films. Walking into a bat cave that creates a giant swarm of bats just isn't going to get you attacked. That's not how their hunting behavior works. Like most wildlife, bats are basically uninterested in interacting with humans. We, on the other hand, have extremely important

reasons to fully study and understand bats, for our sake and theirs. The variety of issues that can occur from direct and indirect contact with bats threaten human lives and bat populations. At the same time, we depend on each other. Safely sharing the planet with bats is a tricky, delicate balance of high importance. So first, let's dive into the basics.

## Bat Basics

Roughly 1,200 species of bats inhabit our planet. That means one out of every five mammal species is a bat! Yet how often do you recall running into one? Probably not many. Maybe you've caught a glimpse of them flying through your vision on a night out under the stars or swiping mosquitoes high above you at dusk, but I'm guessing not much more. Most of that is because they come out mainly at night and are exceptionally good at flying around unnoticed.

Bats range from the size of your thumb to huge, winged flying foxes with wingspans of almost six feet!

Most bats eat insects or fruit. These two diets give bats a crucial role in our ecosystem. They eat a stunning amount and variety of insect pests. That means they save us serious money by keeping many pests from destroying the nation's crops. A group of scientists at Boston University calculated that American farmers save anywhere from $3.7 to $54 billion a year in essential pesticide use simply because of these winged mammals!

In addition to eating insects that could harm crops, bats are extremely important as pollinators. They help pollinate night-blooming flowers and are responsible for pollinating over three hundred types of fruit. Fruits like the dragon fruit and those from the famous saguaro cactus depend solely on bats for pollination—no other animals can pollinate them!

Other bats feed on fish, frogs, lizards, and even other bats! Amazingly, many of these bats are super-specialized to feed on specific animal groups like this.

Simply put, bats are awesome, and we need them. If you have a fear that bats will go out of their way to harm you, I'm guessing it comes from the way they are portrayed in film and television—like *Dracula,* movies where the vampires sparkle—and even the scene in the '80s classic *The Goonies* where Martha Plimpton is screaming about rabies as bats fly around the kids in a cave. Those are, of course, all fiction and not strongly rooted in scientific fact...but it turns out that the myth of vampires does stem from a little bit of reality.

First of all, there are a few bats (the vampire bats) that drink blood. This propensity for the life-giving force of other's blood is known as hematophagy. It's also a fun word to use next time you're at a party!

Vampire bats are the only bats in the world that drink blood! Don't worry—they *generally* don't prefer to drink human blood over that of other animals. But, like most animals, they are opportunistic when it comes to an available food source—so they can definitely drink your blood. In total, there are three species of vampire bats that are known to drink the blood of humans. Even though it is extremely rare and conditions would have to be just right for it to occur, part of the vampire myth surely came from bizarre events of bats feeding on humans.

VAMPIRE
BAT
RANGE

Most of the time, vampire bats get a meal from a larger herbivore, like a goat, cow, sheep, or horse. They sneak up on their sleeping prey by crawling on the ground—it's quieter that way. Once they get close, they use heat-sensing organs in their nose to find where the veins and arteries are near the surface. They have sharp teeth to shear away the hair that's in the way. Then they make a small incision in the skin with their needle-like teeth.

Once the cut is made, they lick the wound. Their saliva is full of powerful anesthetics that dull the pain (so their prey doesn't feel the bite), and blood thinners that keep the blood flowing. In fact, this anticoagulant property in their saliva is super valuable to us. Doctors now use synthetically produced versions of these compounds to reduce blood clotting in stroke patients.

A vampire bat is so good at feeding unnoticed that it can feed for up to thirty minutes at a time. And, fortunately, a bite here or there isn't going to take enough blood to kill anyone. The real problem is that bats are the perfect transmitters of other diseases. In the case of the vampire bats, the concern is rabies.

# Rabies

It's estimated that about 0.5 percent of all bats carry rabies. That's one in two hundred! While that may sound small, it's high enough that you have to be very careful interacting with wild bats. Fortunately, bats with rabies rarely transmit it to people, as they're often quite disoriented and have a hard time flying. That means you don't have to worry about a rogue bat falling from the sky, biting you, and giving you rabies. But it's also why researchers who handle bats take serious precautions, like getting a rabies vaccine before doing field work. It's also why you do not want to pick up or handle a bat on your own. The potential for disease transmission is just too high to take the risk.

# Ebola

After the 1995 Hollywood film *Outbreak,* the deadly Ebola virus claimed infamy on the world stage. There is some evidence that bats may actually be the original hosts of Ebola. Ebola Virus Disease kills up to 90 percent of humans infected by it, and in spite of humanity's efforts, there is no known cure. If you contract the virus without having gotten the newly developed vaccine, only supportive treatment can be offered.

# Other Viruses

Bats are currently known to carry 137 viruses. Of those, we know of 61 viruses that can transfer to other species, such as humans (known as zoonotic viruses). They can carry Nipah, Marburg, SARS, and various coronaviruses. Covid-19 most likely was carried by bats first, although as of the publication of this book, we're still unsure where that virus came from.

Part of what makes them great hosts for viruses is that bats love hanging out in groups. Most infected bats don't die, so they can live long, healthy lives—all the while transferring viruses to other bats. Humans can be infected by many of these viruses through direct contact or (more commonly) through the ingestion of food or water that has been contaminated. An example of this might be a water source that is contaminated by bat feces (guano)—many animals could drink from that source. If those animals are consumed by humans, the virus can be contracted and begin to spread.

# Histoplasmosis (Cave Disease)

The other big problem is that bat droppings are the perfect place for a fungus known as *Histoplasma capsulatum* to grow. Histoplasmosis is a lung disease caused by infection with this fungus. Symptoms are similar to pneumonia. You can definitely treat it, but untreated chronic pulmonary histoplasmosis has a death rate of up to 50 percent.

Even though our relationship is complicated, being scared of bats or getting rid of all of them is never the answer—not even close. Instead, possibly the best thing we can do is to leave bats alone. They can't transfer diseases to us if we don't get ourselves in close contact with them and hold livestock-raising practices to a high standard of safety.

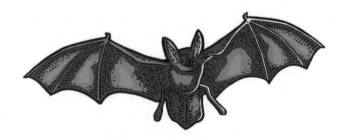

# Scenarios to Avoid

💧 **Avoid going into dusty bat caves** without proper masks and protection.

💧 **Don't handle a live bat** if you don't have training, and especially if you don't have a rabies shot and protective gloves. In many countries, you need a license or permit to handle bats. It's both to limit disease spread and to keep the bats safe.

💧 **Don't eat bats.** Bats are eaten in many places in the world, but the risk of direct transmission of a viral disease is too great, in the opinion of some medical experts. No bat-on-a-stick for me!

# How to Make It Better

💧 We should support making it illegal to farm or consume live bats to help limit the spread of these diseases. Yes, this is a thing.

💧 On a similar note, don't support illegal markets that move living or dead bats around the country. There is currently no definitive evidence that links Covid-19 to bats, but we know there is potential transmission, so why risk it?

# The Most Dangerous

The closest thing to a dangerous bat is a rabid vampire bat or a bat full of viruses. In both cases, it's really not the bat that's dangerous, but what's inside the bat. Again, the thing that really makes bats potentially harmful is that they happen to be great vectors for disease.

# How to Avoid an Attack

Since the three vampire bat species are the only ones that may take a meal from a human, the key is to avoid the very specific circumstances that would allow this rare event to occur. The vampire bat's main prey is cattle in Central and South America, so I highly recommend not sleeping next to a cow or goat at night in the tropics. In fact, if you're near a ranch, make sure you're sleeping inside or with a mosquito net. This is just common sense to prevent an assortment of critters from biting you in this area of the world. Too easy!

# Moose

Let me start by reminding you that a moose is not a predator.
We don't have rogue moose that are *out to get you*. But,
believe it or not, there are way more injuries every year from
moose than from bears and wolves combined.

# The Basics

The moose is the largest deer species in the world. The heaviest moose ever recorded weighed 1,800 pounds and stood seven feet tall at the shoulders. Add to that the head and antlers and it can tower to a height of ten feet. Imagine startling that massive creature in a willow thicket—I should know, it's scary. In fact, startling a giant bull moose in a willow thicket was my first introduction to moose in Alaska.

I was going for a hike with my buddy in this dense bushy wetland. We couldn't see anything, as the willow shrubs were well over our heads. Then, unexpectedly, we heard what sounded to me like a truck plowing through the grass. All I saw was a glimpse of a giant brown mass. We both moved out of the way, and barely missed getting run over as it crossed our path. Did we do the right thing, or did we just get lucky?

To understand moose, you have to understand its place in the ecosystem. It's big, but it has predators. It's a prey species, like deer, squirrels, or cows. That means they're timid by nature and spook easily. Yet, because of their size, they have a tremendous ability to protect themselves.

If moose are aggressive toward humans, it is usually when they feel threatened. If a moose wanders into your backyard, it could be startled by a barking dog running toward it. Instinctually, the moose may treat the dog and any humans nearby just like a threat that would occur in the wild. It may react to you and your dog the same way they react to a wolf attack—the moose will turn to defend itself. Often this means a swift attack to ward off the supposed predator. It'll lower its head and charge. Often the kicking of the feet is what hits you first.

During the fall mating season, in late September to October, bull moose can be particularly aggressive to humans. This is partly because their natural aggression is bolstered by an increase in testosterone. Testosterone is an anabolic steroid, so when animals are souped-up on this stuff, think along the lines of a bodybuilder with 'roid rage.

In the spring, cow moose with calves can be aggressive as they attempt to protect their young from anyone who comes too close. It's a motherly instinct that all mammal mothers have. In moose, it's certainly amplified, because they're big!

# Scenarios to Avoid

- Don't approach a moose closely.

- Don't walk between a mom and her babies.

- Don't walk near a bull moose in the fall mating season.

- Don't feed a moose. This increases the chances that it will charge people—including children. Feeding animals also habituates them, which increases their chance of becoming a "problem animal" that will be killed for human safety.

# Learn the Signs of a Likely Attack

Learning the signs of a likely attack is key to quickly getting to safety. The following behaviors usually accompany attacks:

- A moose will have its back hair raised.
- It will pin its ears back.
- It will lick its snout or smack its lips and teeth.
- It will show the whites in its eyes.
- The moose will lower its head and walk toward you.

# The Most Dangerous

The most dangerous moose is the one you hit in with your car on the highway. In fact, a crash with a moose in a car is thirteen times more likely to end in your death than if you hit a deer. In Alaska alone, there are over eight hundred collisions with moose a year.

# How to Survive a Moose Attack

◊ Don't fight back—you won't win, and it'll just keep fighting you.

◊ Keep dogs away from moose.

◊ Back away or run! You can't fully outrun a moose, so you need to find cover quickly.

◊ Try to get behind a tree, a vehicle, or some other solid object.

◊ If it knocks you down, curl up into a ball and play dead. This position will help protect your head and organs.

◊ Don't get up until it has left the area or it may attack again. Remember, it's not trying to eat you, just neutralize the threat.

# Hippos

Hippos gained a reputation as gentle giants in early media portrayals. They were generally seen as slow, sluggish, peaceful herbivores that loll around in the water their whole lives. In Disney's *Fantasia*, they're shown as clumsy ballerinas...but nothing could be further from the truth!

These massive beasts are, in fact, **the deadliest large land mammal** on earth. They're responsible for killing about five hundred people a year in Africa!

# The Basics

Hippos are remarkable creatures. They look like aquatic cows, but they are actually more closely related to pigs. They are the fifth-largest land mammal, after the three species of elephant and the white rhino.

These semi-aquatic mammals can reach a height of 5.2 feet and a length of 16.5 feet and can weigh 9,900 pounds. At this size, there isn't anything that can eat them! Even full-sized Nile crocodiles (the dinosaur-like mega-reptiles) are no match for a full-grown hippo. There is no doubt that their aggressive nature is part of what has allowed them to successfully coexist with crocodiles and other African predators.

The hippo has a unique set of teeth, as well. For an animal that typically eats vegetation, the teeth are oddly inappropriate for foraging grass. Instead, they tout giant canines that look more like those of a saber-toothed cat. These teeth are used in aggressive displays and to fend off invaders. At over a foot and a half long, these teeth are extremely effective!

Typically, a hippo eats grass along the shore at night, but they're not just herbivores. They've been known to kill impala, kudu, eland, wildebeest, and buffalo on occasion. There is evidence that they not only occasionally eat meat, but are predators too. It has even been reported that they occasionally eat each other! Fortunately for us, they don't seem to hunt and eat humans, but death by hippo is far too common.

In 2014, as an example, a small boat full of school children was attacked by a hippo. Thirteen school kids and one teacher died in the incident. As far as I can tell from the report, the deaths didn't result in the hippo eating the individuals, but they died nonetheless. Attacks like this are unfortunately what make hippos the deadliest large mammal on the planet.

Hippos are also known to wander out of the water to forage on vegetation. They eat about eighty pounds of grass a night, so they can quickly deplete their local food sources. Scientists have tracked them traveling a kilometer or more a night looking for food.

Roaming activity like this has put them into conflict with humans. They've been seen chasing cattle and other large mammals. They also enjoy eating human crops.

# Scenarios to Avoid

Ideally, you'll want to avoid a hippo both on land and in water. That means you need to keep alert when you're near a waterway. Looking for hippo signs—like poop and footprints—is a good start.

**Don't sneak up on a hippo.** Save your "sneaking" for mega-predatory animals like lions, wolves, or polar bears who, if they see you, might want to eat you. Let hippos know you're there. Hippos can remain underwater for six minutes or more. If you are swimming in the water or are in a small boat and see a hippo surface far from you, slap the water continuously with an object like a paddle. This will alert the hippos to your presence and decrease the likelihood they might accidentally surface next to you. Don't slap with your hands if you can help it—crocodiles (which are found near hippos) are attracted to splashing, and they love hands!

**A "yawning" or "laughing" hippo is a sign of aggression** that could precede an attack.

**On land, don't get between a hippo and the water.**

**Shallow water is a bad place to be**. Hippos don't actually swim—they bounce off the bottom in a body of water. So in this case, deeper water would be safer.

**Avoid mating season.** It's the worst time to encounter a hippo because the males are even more aggressive.

**Stay away from calves.** Angry mothers are no fun and highly aggressive.

# The Most Dangerous

The most dangerous thing you can do is navigate a waterway that is choked with numerous hippos—especially in the dry season. Give them space. It is in their nature to defend their territory.

# How to Survive an Up-Close Hippo Encounter

- If a hippo opens its mouth to flash its teeth, **flee** immediately.

- If you're in the water, **move in the opposite direction** of where you saw the hippos.

- If you're on land, **find cover.** You can't outrun a hippo in a straight line, so find a tree, rock, or vehicle to get between you and the hippo. This will help slow the attack and perhaps help you get safely to shelter.

🔥 **Run in a zigzag if you have to.** The mass of a hippo makes it difficult for them to change direction, so "faking them out" by quickly changing directions can work in your favor long enough to get to safety.

**Fun Hippo Fact**

Pablo Escobar, the world's most infamous Colombian drug runner, imported hippos from Africa to live in his backyard. Some of them escaped, and they're now an invasive species in the Amazon! There are reportedly between forty and sixty hippos presently roaming the jungle.

# Mosquitoes

Have you ever wondered what would happen if you took a cage of roughly two thousand mosquitoes and stuck your hand inside? If you're like most of the people that I described one of my latest videos to, you probably haven't. I had always wanted to do this, however, and finally got my chance when I was visiting the University of Florida's Entomology and Nematology Department.

The video was all about how to protect yourself from mosquitoes, so over the two months I worked on the film, I became my own mini-expert on the topic. It blew my mind that, in the past, researchers would rear mosquitoes on their own blood. It was a tried-and-true technique that is only now falling out of fashion.

I felt certain I wouldn't get a disease from these captive-bred mosquitoes, because mosquitoes generally don't pass diseases to their offspring. I also knew that only the females would be feeding—essentially getting a blood meal to nourish their developing eggs. What I didn't anticipate, though, was that after having mosquitoes suck my blood for about fifteen minutes, my body would have an unexpected immune response to the bites, and I'd end up in bed for most of the following day.

# The Basics

It's surprising to most people that the deadliest animal in the world is actually the mosquito, but numbers don't lie. Mosquitoes are responsible for around a million deaths a year, but (unless you have a rare allergy) mosquitoes themselves are not what can actually kill you. In fact, and speaking from a highly uncomfortable personal experience in a mosquito lab, even a couple thousand mosquito bites at once won't really harm you beyond the normal itching and red bumps! Instead, deaths occur because mosquitoes can carry some of the worst disease-causing pathogens on earth. Fortunately, having just a bit of knowledge means we can do something about it!

Not everyone is aware that there are lots of species of mosquitoes. Worldwide, there are more than three thousand. Each mosquito adult is specialized to feed on a particular kind of host. The larvae are specialized to live in specific aquatic environments and feed on specific organisms. Not all adults feed on blood, but among blood-feeders, it is only the adult females that take a blood meal. So, if you get one of these bloodsuckers on your arm, you know it's a soon-to-be mom. She needs your blood to nourish all the eggs she will lay!

Some species of blood-sucking mosquitoes feed on birds, some on frogs, some on lizards, and some on earthworms. A select few will bite humans, and a few of those are really well-adapted to living near human developments. They belong to the genera *Aedes*, *Culex*, and *Anopheles*. These are the mosquitoes we need to focus on if we're going to prevent the deadly diseases they carry.

# The Diseases

The destructive diseases mosquitoes carry are referred to as *mosquito-borne pathogens*. In some cases they are protozoa, like malaria. In others, it's a virus, like in Zika or yellow fever. It could even be a worm, like the worm that causes elephantiasis. But it doesn't end there. Mosquitoes can even carry the eggs of botflies that can be transferred to your skin when bitten. The botfly eggs hatch into minuscule larvae that can burrow under your skin and eat your flesh. Once one matures, it breaks back through your dermis and emerges as a fat, writhing, worm-like botfly larva! Ew.

**Here is a list of some of the worst diseases caused by mosquito pathogens, for reference:**

- Malaria
- Zika
- Dengue fever
- West Nile virus
- Chikungunya
- Yellow fever
- Various types of encephalitis
- Tularemia
- Dirofilariasis

# How Mosquitoes Spread These Diseases

In almost all known cases, a freshly hatched mosquito does not have any of these diseases. I say *most* because there are always exceptions to the rule. Instead, the main way diseases are transmitted is when a mosquito takes a blood meal from an infected host and carries that pathogen to another host. Because of this pathway, the mosquito is just the vector of the actual killing agent. Thus, the mosquito takes the title of deadliest animal only because it's good at assisting other organisms in killing us.

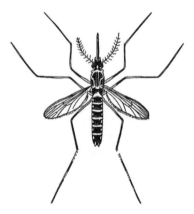

To prevent transmission, we have to prevent mosquitoes from biting us. Here are a few ways to stop transmission.

1.  **Make sure infected people don't get bitten**. Essentially quarantine people who are infected with mosquito-borne disease indoors or, as is done in areas outside the US, under mosquito nets. If they are bitten, the mosquito can continue to spread the pathogen.

2.  **Limit your possibility of being bitten** by wearing insect repellant and long-sleeved clothes. Spending time

indoors in areas with screens or sleeping under mosquito nets also limits interaction with mosquitoes. Mosquito-borne illnesses aren't everywhere, but this is really important when you're in any area where these diseases are found.

3. **Spray for adult mosquitoes.** Mosquito control can target adult mosquitoes by spraying with certain concentrations of insecticide at certain times of day. In fact, by keeping populations of mosquitoes low, it reduces the likelihood of disease transmission.

4. **Kill the larvae.** Adult mosquitoes come from larvae that live in water bodies, so finding ways to kill or prevent them is helpful. This might include getting rid of water-holding containers around the home, treating that water with larvicide, or using mosquito fish to eat the mosquito larvae. All of those are really effective.

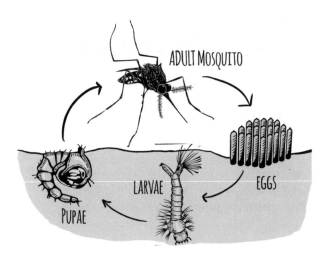

Getting rid of water-holding containers where mosquito larvae develop is the most effective way to get rid of problem mosquitoes. In fact, two of the mosquitoes that are most problematic for humans—two species in the genus *Aedes*—don't travel far from their hatching location. They may only go a city block or two from where they hatched. That means, if you can get rid of standing water around your home, you'll go far in getting rid of these mosquitoes.

Most people don't realize that water bodies can be created from a ton of things in their yard. Tarps collect water when lying on the ground. Kids' toys do the same—an upside-down Frisbee with water in it is enough to create a large number of mosquitoes. Even spare tires and trash can be breeding grounds for mosquitoes. Spend some time looking around your yard after a rain. If anything has water in it, find a way to tip it or turn it over. I cannot overstress that getting rid of even tiny pools of water near your home is the most effective way to keep your yard as mosquito-free as possible. It works!

# Scenarios to Avoid

- 🔥 Having standing water in containers outdoors

- 🔥 Sleeping outdoors without a net

- 🔥 Walking around without applying insect repellant in areas with lots of known mosquito-borne illnesses

- 🔥 Going to areas that have high rates of mosquito-borne illness without getting the proper vaccines

# The Most Dangerous Disease

Mosquitoes carry some really bad disease-causing pathogens. Dengue (or breakbone fever), yellow fever, Zika (which causes babies to have small heads), and West Nile, to name a few. But the worst is malaria.

**Malaria** is the deadliest disease known to humans and is carried by female *Anopheles* mosquitoes. It has even halted armies throughout history. It infected Theodore Roosevelt, George Washington, Abraham Lincoln, and John F. Kennedy. Astoundingly, it is suspected that half of all humans that ever lived died of this disease. Malaria is the reason the CDC (the Centers for Disease Control and Prevention) was created in the US in 1946. It was also one of the reasons it took so long to build the Panama Canal—they couldn't keep laborers well enough to complete it. Americans don't think about it much because it's been mostly eradicated from the Western world, but it is still prevalent in other parts of the world. When traveling to areas with high malaria rates, you can take preventative malaria medication before you even leave. This not only protects you, but also prevents the spread of this terrible disease.

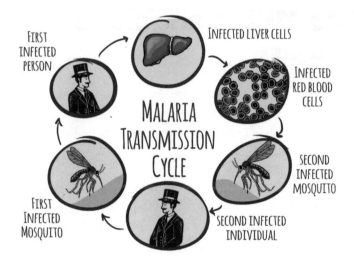

First Infected Person

Infected Liver Cells

Infected Red Blood Cells

MALARIA Transmission Cycle

Second Infected Mosquito

First Infected Mosquito

Second Infected Individual

# How to Survive the Mosquito

First, I'll reiterate that it's basically impossible for a mosquito alone to kill a person. The pathogens are what kill people. How you survive after getting infected is different for each illness, and I'd need another entire book to cover how you'd recover from those. Just keep in mind that everyone has a role to play in stopping these illnesses. You can eliminate any non-natural water catchments where mosquitoes can develop and get all necessary vaccinations and medication when you travel abroad.

# The Take-Home

I should note that, while mosquito pathogens could be transferred just about anywhere their host mosquito lives, many places in the world have done a tremendous job of eradicating the diseases. Florida is a great case in point. The entire state is swampy and full of mosquitoes. Without the concerted efforts of mosquito control and the general public's support, diseases like malaria, yellow fever, dengue, and Zika would be far more prevalent than they are. Fortunately, scientists make sure those diseases are quickly quashed every time they pop up in the state. These creative and passionate entomologists are keeping everyone safer, shielding us from threats we might never know existed if they do their job well!

# Elephants

On one filming trip to Africa, Haley and I slept in a canvas tent within a protected camp that was then surrounded by electric fencing. In the morning, we were awakened by the local guards who informed us that elephants had destroyed the fence in the night. They essentially said they now had an *elephant problem* and we were advised to move to the second camp. While I knew little about elephants at that time, I could sense from the tone of their voice that the situation was serious. On the way out I looked at the fence. The elephants had cleverly pulled up the posts of the fence without touching the electrified wires. This was my first look at just how powerful and intelligent these wild animals are when interacting with humans.

With the exception of hippos, crocodiles, and possibly African buffalo, elephants kill more people than any other large land mammal. On average, they're responsible for close to five hundred deaths a year. Should you find yourself in the bush and in a face-off with an angry elephant, it's probably a good idea that you don't make the situation even worse than it is.

# The Basics

Elephants are the largest land animal on earth. The largest elephant ever weighed in at 24,000 pounds. It was a large male African elephant, with a shoulder height of thirteen feet and giant eleven-foot tusks. The three living species of elephants evolved in Africa and Asia, not only with deadly predators like lions and tigers...but also with humans!

That means they have a long history of learning through trial and error how to survive in their habitats alongside some very formidable foes. They're fully capable of living with us in part because of their ability to fight back with great force if needed. Unfortunately they can't fight back against heavy artillery, helicopters, and other high tech that poachers use to hunt and kill elephants. Consequently, these mighty creatures are threatened or endangered throughout their range.

Until recently there were two species of elephants: African and Asian. Based on genetic evidence, scientists now also distinguish smaller forest elephants as a unique species. For our purposes, I am lumping all elephants together. They share similar enough behaviors that learning how to deal with one will help you with the others, too.

The first thing to understand in all of this is that elephants are really intelligent—among the most intelligent creatures on the planet. They learn from their interactions in the wild and with humans. They've also evolved beside humans in both Africa and Asia. Unlike the now-extinct mammoths and mastodons, which evolved in their North American range mostly without humans, elephants have found an aggressive way to sustain their way of life and family structure.

Elephants are big and have a ton of power. They could crush most foes without much struggle, but they have developed a defensive strategy to avoid unnecessary conflict. I have observed elephants in the wild countless times, watching them go about in a peaceful way with their family group. They are certainly not *out to get you*, so to speak. In fact, they're generally only aggressive when heavily poached. With all of this in mind, we can set the stage for interacting with elephants by examining a few behaviors and one defensive strategy—the charge!

With elephants, there are basically two types of charges—*bluff* charges and *attack* charges. These are two very different things, and we'll tackle the differences here.

# Bluff Charges

Bluff charges are meant simply to stop a threat from advancing any further. The elephant wants you to know it means business but isn't going to actually attack you. Its ears will be fanned out wide, making it appear larger. It will sway from side to side, pivoting from one leg to the other, doing what are known as "displacement activities." Its trunk will not be pinned up and under its body but will instead be swaying from side to side or hanging down below the head.

# Attack Charges

In an actual charge, where the elephant runs at you to trample and impale you with its tusks, this will all be preceded by very different display behavior. Its ears will be pinned back on its head. The trunk will be curled up under it and turned inward. The elephant won't display the "displacement activities" that are mostly used to bluff charge. You'll want to run!

# Scenarios to Avoid

If you see a herd of elephants from afar, you should keep your distance and give them plenty of space. However, there are a few particular scenarios that are even more prudent to avoid.

- **Bulls during musth**—they are full of testosterone and extra aggressive.

- **Don't sneak up on a herd.** Nobody likes getting spooked, and a scared elephant is prone to charge.

- **Don't threaten or approach a baby elephant.** This probably seems obvious, but herds fiercely protect their young and will take extraordinary measures to make sure they're safe.

- **Keep food away from your dwelling.** Food might entice a hungry elephant to come too close, and driving away hungry elephants while they're feasting makes for unhappy elephants!

# The Most Dangerous

The most dangerous situation is to encounter an aggressive or aggravated elephant—essentially an elephant that isn't interested in just bluff-charging you. Elephants can get mad for a variety of reasons, just as humans get mad on bad days. For instance, they may have encountered poachers in their last human interaction, and that could influence their behavior. They could also be hungry, hurt, or scared. You definitely don't want to spook an elephant! Whatever the cause, you especially want to avoid these massive (up to twelve-ton) mammals when they are not behaving in their typical calm manner.

# How to Survive an Elephant Attack

If an elephant does attack-charge you, it will use its tusks to gore you, throw you, and crush you. It will often keep stomping until you're dead. Since elephants can plow down trees, flip cars, and run up to twenty-five miles an hour, you have little chance of outrunning them. So your best bet is to read the signals early and recognize whether you are seeing a bluff charge or a real charge. Here is what you do in each case.

If you read the body language and believe it's a **bluff charge,** do the following:

1.  **Stay calm.** This sounds counterintuitive.

2.  **Show them you're not a threat.** Remember, they're smart and, if they're exposed to humans regularly, they can read your body language. This means talking in a soft voice, not waving your hands or beating your chest. If all goes well, the elephant will stop any bluff charge behaviors and eventually appear calm.

3.  **Give them space.** Remember, the elephant just wants you out of its personal space. It doesn't mean you need to run. I suppose if you can run and you're wearing good sneakers, maybe go for that.

4.  If they keep approaching in spite of your calm, **yelling becomes an option** here. It shows that you are not intimidated and could be a threat yourself if they approach further. Let's hope this is as far as it gets.

If it's **not a bluff charge**, you're in serious trouble. This is what you're best advised to do:

1.  **Run**—and run in a zigzag pattern. This utilizes your smaller mass. Hopefully they can't change direction as fast as you.

2.  **Get a large object between you and the elephant**—the bigger the better. Don't forget that they can flip cars and plow through small shrubs.

3.  **Don't climb a tree** unless it's a massive tree. Let's face it, that tree will have to be really big or the elephant will just knock it down. Plus, so many of the trees in Africa are full of thorns. You're better off using your energy running.

**Fun Fact**

Elephants are actually really scared of bees. If you have enough forethought, you might want to carry a big speaker system equipped with African bee sounds! Studies have shown they'll back down if this sound is played. Even elephants with thick skin make it a high priority to avoid getting stung.

# Bison

There's not much that is more iconic of the American West than seeing large herds of bison roaming the prairie, and you can see them for yourself if you visit Yellowstone National Park. As a grad student in wildlife filmmaking, I lived only forty-five minutes from the park entrance, and I definitely took advantage of it. Much of my first year was consumed by making one film called *Death in Yellowstone*. What I observed during the filmmaking process was that, while more people are fearful of grizzlies, black bears, and mountain lions, it's bison that are arguably even more dangerous. It's not because they're *out to get you*—but because people seem to have forgotten how formidable these grazing herbivores can be when they're approached by humans.

**WARNING**

**Many visitors have been gored by buffalo**

These animals may appear tame but are wild, unpredictable, and dangerous

**DO NOT APPROACH BUFFALO**

StoneAgeMan.com

# The Basics

American bison, sometimes called (incorrectly) the buffalo, used to roam North America from coast to coast, grazing throughout the vast temperate grasslands. They are herbivores that got really good at defending themselves from wolves, cougars, saber-toothed cats, and (later) American Indians.

Bison were in no way able to adapt to life with firearms. Because of hunting with firearms, fewer than four hundred remained at the end of the nineteenth century! Fortunately, the population has rebounded in many areas, and visitors to Yellowstone can view these impressive creatures grazing the landscape. The only time bison seem to take defensive action toward humans is when an uninformed tourist breaks the rules and gets too close. If a person gets hurt or killed by a bison, it is almost certainly because they have made the choice to walk right up to this wild animal.

I think people get lulled into a sense of security with bison because they might think of them as big, furry cows. Let me assure you, they are not. Bison have survived so long on the planet because they are huge, aggressive beasts with giant pointy horns on their head. The largest bull ever recorded weighed 2,800 pounds. They often stand six feet high at the shoulder and can reach almost twelve feet in length! Their horns are sharp and can be two feet long. They are also surprisingly quick on their feet. An adult bison can run at speeds up to forty miles per hour.

In many of the places where bison have rebounded, they have become somewhat habituated to humans and don't see them as a threat. But that's not always the case. They have evolved instinctive behaviors to defend themselves and their young from threats like wolves, so one of the most important things you can do is to make sure you don't resemble a predator and trigger a defensive attack.

# Scenarios to Avoid

Here are a few recommendations that can save your life. These may seem like common sense, but they are based on tragic events in documented scenarios.

- 🔥 **Don't try to take a selfie with a bison** behind you.

- 🔥 **Don't sneak up on a bison**. As herbivores, they're the prey in their habitat, and they don't like getting spooked.

- 🔥 **Avoid walking through a giant meadow with a bison herd in it**. It leaves you with no place to shelter should they turn on you and stampede.

- 🔥 **Dogs should be leashed.** Remember, dogs are basically wolves to a bison—and wolves are their main predator. If a dog starts barking and chasing a bison, it could trigger the defensive behavior that may ultimately get you mixed in.

- 🔥 **Don't feed a wild bison.** That gets you way too close to their horns.

- 🔥 **Don't get close to a calf.** In May and June, cows are super protective of their young.

- 🔥 **Don't get near an aggressive male**. In July and August, bulls are full of testosterone and will charge at just about anything.

# The Most Dangerous

The most dangerous bison is one that is displaying warning signs—so let's go through a few of those. This may take the form of snorting, shaking the head from side to side, pawing at the ground, raising the tail or even bluff-charging—running or turning quickly toward you as a warning. Think about a bull in a bull-fighting ring—stomping its front hooves, lowering its head, and generally looking mean. If the bison is doing anything that looks like that, you're in trouble.

# How to Survive an Attack

Let's say you're on a stroll through the prairie in Yellowstone or another wilderness area with bison, and you've somehow missed the signs that bison are around. Clearly you wouldn't have gone up to one to take a selfie, yet now you're in a predicament. You're face-to-face with a big hoofed mammal with horns. What do you do? Here is a decent plan to survive:

- **Back away slowly** if you can. If you're in a big field, running isn't going to help. They can run up to forty miles per hour.

- **Find an obstacle**—something to put between you and the bison. In other words, you should run to a big boulder, a vehicle, or even a group of trees if possible.

- **Get up a tree if there is one nearby**—they can't climb, so you might be safe.

# The Take-Home

If you visit a place like Yellowstone that has giant herds of bison roaming between cars, don't be fooled. While you may only see the nonaggressive interactions in a brief time observing them, know that they're not tame. Bison can quickly see you as a threat and turn on you. Nobody wants to get gored with a horn, and it's fairly easy to keep that from happening if you give them some space. You have probably noticed a theme emerging— they're not *out to get you.*

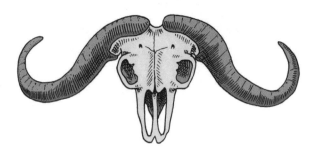

# Whales

I've had two interactions with whales and dolphins that I will never forget. The first was a close call with a humpback whale at midnight while sailing between the islands of Hawaii. I was in a small sailboat with my best friend and a humpback surfaced literally inches from our boat. Had it been a few feet over, we might well have overturned that small boat and been left helpless in the vastness of the ocean, due to a mere accidental bump by one of earth's largest creatures.

The other was in Tasmania, on an isolated sandy beach. I was with a friend when we spotted a pod of dolphins a hundred yards or so offshore. Without thinking, we jumped into the chilly water and swam out toward them. I mostly assumed they'd just swim away, but they did the opposite. The entire pod turned and made a beeline right for us. At the last minute they turned and bumped me in the chest. Frankly it scared me a lot! Dolphins look really gentle on the horizon, but a massive dolphin that is swimming right at you is a totally different story. They stuck around for maybe thirty seconds, enough to get bored, and then swam away again. It was an amazing experience that made me appreciate them in an entirely new way. Not everyone in history has viewed dolphins and whales like this, though.

Imagine for a second that you live in the eighteenth century. The seas are a wild and untamed frontier full of dangerous creatures. All you know of whales is from reading the account of the white whale in *Moby-Dick*. Maybe you also know the Old Testament account of Jonah, who was literally swallowed by a whale. From these stories alone, you may get the biased impression that whales are extremely dangerous beasts of the sea.

Fortunately, we have much more accurate information to guide our opinion about whales today! Modern Sea World shows, aquariums, BBC specials like *Blue Planet*, and current bans on whaling have changed most people's views of whales. Maybe our view now is a bit more aligned with the truth about these huge animals. Whales are beautiful, massive, and extremely intelligent, so it's worth sorting the truth from the fiction.

# The Basics

There are ninety species of whales and dolphins, which collectively we call cetaceans. They range from the tiny 4.5-foot vaquita to the massive blue whale. Blue whales are the largest animals to have ever lived on this planet. An adult blue whale can weigh 190 tons and reach 110 feet long—which, for perspective, is about three school buses end to end! In fact, we should feel pretty lucky that (1) we live in this time and can witness them and (2) that we didn't hunt them to extinction... because that did nearly happen.

Most whales eat very small prey, from tiny fish to small shrimp-like organisms like krill. They filter-feed on these organisms from the ocean. Because of this diet and the fact that they didn't evolve with humans in any practical sense, these whales aren't interested in humans other than out of curiosity when we show up.

I suppose, in theory, they could engulf a human in their mouths, but they'd never get them into their stomachs. Their throats are very small due to what they normally eat.

This very fact seems to put the story of Jonah and the whale in a very different context. The story is more likely a metaphor about battling your demons than about actually battling a real whale. But let's just say for a second that it was. What whale would it have been? It has to be a whale capable of swallowing a human.

This is when the sperm whale stories start to get interesting. *Moby-Dick*, for instance, is a fictional story that apparently came from two true events. One was a tale of a legendary white whale that was spotted by sailors. (A white whale is significant because most sperm whales are gray.) The story of a whale sinking a ship came from George Pollard. In 1820, he captained the whaling ship *Essex*, which was rammed and sunk by a sperm whale. The small crew was stranded at sea a thousand-plus miles from the nearest land. They resorted to cannibalism, and Pollard barely lived to tell their tale. No doubt, the sperm whale didn't take too kindly to whatever they were up to. That seems fair on the part of the whale. Then you add to these stories the fact the sperm whale is one of only a few whales that have large throats...

You read that right. Sperm whales have large throats.

That means they can eat bigger prey—most notably, giant squid. With that nugget of truth in your pocket, you could very easily imagine a story where a whale could sink a boat and swallow a person. But the fact is that, so far, we have no valid accounts of a sperm whale ever having eaten a human. In fact, sperm whales seem to be gentle giants who find humans rather interesting.

Mind you, whales are intelligent and can learn from their experiences. If, for instance, the last encounter a sperm whale had was with a whaling vessel that either killed or injured a family member, it will treat the next human the same. This may be what happened with the whale George Pollard encountered that became the basis for *Moby-Dick*. Fortunately for us today, we don't generally hunt whales. So most whales only see us as curiosities. I've talked with countless biologists who've been in the water with them, and many say whales are very curious and even go so far as to call them kind. Some have recounted the whales actually trying to protect them from a true whale-enemy, the shark.

Killer whales, aka orcas, also have larger throats. Many eat seals and other marine mammals that are actually much bigger than humans. In theory, they too could eat a human. But, as of 2020, there have been no reports of wild orcas ever killing a human. Currently there are only a handful of reports of encounters or "attacks" on humans. Those few usually result in the whale grabbing a person briefly and then releasing them. There are, however, four well-known incidents of orcas in captivity killing humans. They never ate the human involved, so, you know, that's good.

In addition to sperm whales and orcas, there are a few incidents of dolphins and pilot whales having grabbed or bumped people in the ocean. While this has caused some injury, it always seems pretty harmless, and most likely the cetacean just doesn't realize its own strength when interacting with our more fragile species.

Still, let's walk through some basic safety tips when dealing with these animals.

# Scenarios to Avoid

I should note before we start that in most areas, it's illegal to jump in the water with marine mammals. Yet, occasionally, you're in the water when they approach you, so it's worth having a plan. Here are some suggestions based on past incidents.

**Don't jump into a tank with any captive whale** if you're not a whale trainer. Two of the four orca-related deaths are linked to bystanders falling into the tank of a captive animal.

**Don't purposely look like a seal.** Orcas, for example, actively hunt seals. Even more so, I suggest not dressing up like a shark and swimming with orcas. That's because we know they attack and kill massive great white sharks. So if that's what you were planning to do, skip it.

**Avoid hopping in the water with them if they're mating.** They're a bit more prone to bump and injure you in this situation. This might be hard to spot if you're a novice. Bottlenose dolphins, for example, do a lot of circling, bullying, and leaping in one spot when mating. Humpbacks do a lot of jumping, and thus, a run-in at this time can be risky.

**Stay clear of whales that are actively feeding.** This goes for all whales and dolphins really. Not only are you getting in the way of a hungry and massive creature that does have a big mouth, but why would you bother them when they're just trying to have a meal? Just stand back a bit and watch.

# The Most Dangerous

A dead whale is actually the most dangerous kind of whale. If the whale is floating at sea, the carcass can attract sharks. On shore, a whale can bloat due to natural bacteria involved in the decomposition process. Their thick blubber makes it difficult for the pressure to be released, until...they literally explode.

In 2013, a dead sperm whale, which had been sitting in the waters around the Faroe Islands for a few days, was finally hauled onto land. When a marine biologist made an incision in its belly to relieve pressure, it literally exploded. Thankfully, the mass of guts missed him, and the YouTube video now lives on in infamy.

In 2004, another sperm whale was stranded on a beach in Taiwan. Researchers wanted to dissect it for educational purposes, so they loaded it on a flatbed and started off to the research station. Unfortunately, during transit, it exploded. It sent a river of blood, intestines, and organs all over the city street! It was supremely gross, and worse, that one didn't even have a viral video associated with it for us to look at later.

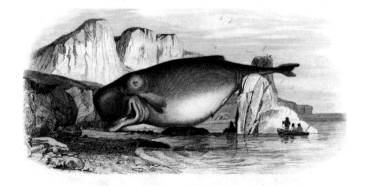

In 1970, humans tried to blow up a gray whale on the beaches of Oregon. (This is my favorite exploding-whale video, by the way.) The explosion sent chunks of whale blubber into the air and hundreds of meters away. Those pieces rained down on bystanders and even destroyed a few cars.

Captive killer whales are generally not dangerous but, given that we interact with them more than wild ones, there are more documented incidents. Only four deaths have been recorded involving captive whales, and three of those are by the same individual whale. People have suggested that some of these captive animals suffer from mental problems due to their captive and confined lifestyles. That seems pretty likely and a good reason to be cautious in these situations and to rethink why we have them in captivity.

# How to Survive an Attack

Given that there are no reports of whales of any kind actually eating a human, you can assume that, if a whale or dolphin somehow grabs you, it's not doing so to eat you. Hooray! But you'll still need to know how to get out of a "grab and go" situation like that. Here are some guidelines to help.

1. **Stay calm**.

2. **Take a deep breath**. If they do grab you and hold you down, chances are you'll get released soon.

3. **Get out of the water** as quickly as possible. If a whale or dolphin does choose to interact in a way that involves grabbing you, this is likely a new interaction for them. They probably don't know their own strength, and it could be pretty dangerous.

I hope this gives you some insight into the cetaceans. Relish any wild interactions you have. They're amazing creatures that we share this earth with. They haven't learned to fear us, and let's hope we keep it that way. We can totally share this planet together and maybe get lucky enough to stare each other in the eye on occasion.

# Non-Human Primates

In 2012, Haley and I made a documentary about scientists who were doing a groundbreaking primate study in Kenya. They were trying to ascertain how the baboon troop made the decision to go from one place to another. To do this, they needed to put the world's most advanced tracking collars on an entire troop—something that had never been done. I sometimes like to tell people that we lived with a troop of baboons for two weeks in Africa, but that's not exactly accurate. We did, however, spend most of our waking hours with them. They were habituated to our presence during feeding times, so they tolerated us quietly filming and observing them as they went about their day. We were working with accomplished researchers, veterinarians, and Kenyan wildlife officials, so we had strict safety procedures in place. We followed them to the letter, because hanging out with baboons carries some serious potential danger.

At any one time, there were about forty olive baboons around us on the ground, feeding. There were large eighty-plus-pound dominant males with massive canines that far outmatched any of us in both speed and strength. Then there were mothers, babies, and a handful of young adults mixed in. The scariest ones, from my perspective, were the huge males who would forcefully come running into the action if other individuals began making an alarm call.

Our instructions from the local guides and scientists were pretty simple:

    &#9679; Arrive before dawn to set out food in the study traps and surrounding areas before the baboons woke up. This was to make sure they could not see us and associate us with a food source or with the study traps.

- Stay calm, stay quiet, and move slowly if at all.

- Don't look them in the eye. Essentially this shows you're not a threat that they need to deal with.

This worked well to get them habituated to our presence so we could put temporary tracking collars on them. Once that began, safety protocol sometimes reverted back to "stay in the truck and let the vets handle it." This was my first introduction to safety protocols around primates.

Primates are the monkeys and apes of the world. They range from small marmosets to huge male gorillas. The great apes have been depicted in Hollywood movies as violent brutes since the beginning of cinema, like *King Kong* for example. It took amazing work by primatologists such as Dian Fossey, Jane Goodall, and others to change our minds a bit. In fact, the modern-day depiction of *King Kong* portrays him more as a hero than a villain. Let's not forget, though, that an interaction with a great ape should not be treated lightly. The largest wild lowland gorillas weigh three to four hundred pounds and are easily ten times stronger than a man.

Are these primates innately dangerous to us? That question was on everyone's mind in 2016 when a boy fell into the gorilla habitat at the Cincinnati Zoo. A 440-pound silverback by the name of Harambe grabbed him after he fell in. Video of the incident shows him at times looking protective, and at other times pulling the kid around almost like a rag doll. Was this a protective and loving behavior, or was it aggressive? The key to knowing that lies in understanding their wild behaviors.

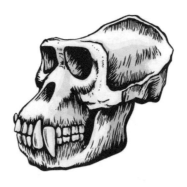

Unfortunately, in this case, zookeepers made the quick decision that this may have been a type of display behavior—something male gorillas do when they feel threatened. To save the boy, the zoo shot and killed Harambe, much to the horror of many. The zoo defended its actions, and to be fair, that's a hard call to make in the chaos that was happening during the event. In hindsight, I've spoken with some of the world's experts in gorilla behavior who think the best option, given the situation, would have been to separate the gorilla from the child.

This may be one of the most important reasons to discuss the behaviors of these animals here. So here is a quick synopsis of what we know about many of the primates and how to deal with a few that could be considered dangerous.

# The Basics

There are around five hundred species of primates. That includes monkeys and what we call the great apes—gorillas, chimpanzees, bonobos, orangutans, and of course, *Homo sapiens*. I'll leave humans out of this treatment, though. We all know we're potentially dangerous.

Of all these, there are only a handful that do more than throw poop at you from the treetops, which has definitely happened to me a few times. Let's briefly go through each—each primate, not each poop-throwing encounter.

# Gorillas

Gorilla troops tend to be generally peaceful. They eat mostly vegetation, and the large males are more defensive than aggressive. They'll tolerate or (more likely) run away from people approaching, so long as you don't seem aggressive to them. I'll go more into avoiding conflict with them later in this chapter.

# Chimpanzees

Chimps share 98 percent of our DNA. They're similar to bonobos, with one main behavioral distinction—they're known to murder their own kind. In fact, scientists have documented 152 murders where one clan of chimps gangs up and kills a member of a nearby group. These attacks aren't always restricted to their own kind. They routinely gang up on other monkeys (mostly red colobus monkeys) to eat them. After trapping these monkeys, they'll dismember and consume body parts, sometimes as the monkey continues to scream. If that thought disturbs you, searching for it on YouTube will definitely give you nightmares.

Occasionally, chimps are violent toward humans. In the mid-1990s, for example, a male chimp by the name of Saddam was terrorizing villages in Uganda. One kid was grabbed from a blanket as the mother was picking crops nearby. Another was taken from a woman's back as she was picking cassava. In total, he attacked seven children and killed at least two of them.

# Orangutans

These great apes are generally very peaceful. They're strong, so you definitely need to be careful around them. Attacks on humans are rare, and there is only one documented case of an orangutan actually killing another orangutan.

You can usually tell when they are upset, since they'll do what's called a kiss squeak and start running away or displaying. You know they're really upset if they "snag crash," which involves pushing dead or dying trees so they fall in your direction. Usually, however, they try to leave before this happens.

# Rhesus Macaques

In India, rhesus monkeys live in giant troops of up to two hundred individuals that are constantly causing problems for humans. They're well-adapted to living near us, and they're good at stealing food. A fair number of problems have arisen when they're in these situations and habituated to humans.

In 2018, for instance, a baby was snatched from a crib and killed. That same year, a troop of macaques was to blame for a bunch of bricks falling on an elderly man and killing him. Even if they're not in the news for killing someone, they're often aggressive toward people and love to steal stuff—"cantankerous little punks," as one researcher I know likes to call them. They are also known to carry herpes B, which isn't dangerous for them, but has an 80 percent mortality rate for humans. That means that even a small bite has the potential to kill you.

# Other Primates That Use Aggression in Lethal Attacks

Lethal attacks targeting other adults within a species are rare. Besides chimps, only orangutans, red colobus monkeys, capuchins, muriquis, and spider monkeys have been observed using deadly force on one another.

With that said, here are a few more monkeys that are large and should command respect:

- Baboons—all five species
- Mandrills and drills
- Geladas
- Spider monkeys
- Macaques
- Langurs

If you've never heard of these, that's okay. I listed them here so you have something fun to look up on YouTube in the future—these primates are incredible!

# Deadly Diseases

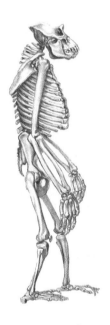

Let's not forget that we're genetically very similar to other primates. This close relationship means a virus that infects another primate could more easily infect us than a distantly related species. They can harbor some dangerous diseases, too. Macaques can carry a deadly form of herpes known as herpes B. They also harbor rabies and Zika. Many species, including baboons and orangutans, are known to have hepatitis, so you don't want to get bitten by one. Hunting and eating chimps and sooty mangabeys in West Africa likely gave rise to HIV in humans. We could also get things like tuberculosis, Ebola, monkeypox, and yellow fever. Plus, there is always the possibility that we could pick up other, yet-unstudied diseases.

# Scenarios to Avoid

**Don't stare at a gorilla, beat your chest, or attack them.**
Flashing teeth and chest beating are signs of dominance in
gorilla hierarchies. You don't want to challenge a gorilla. You
won't win.

**Don't leave a baby or young child unattended near chimps or
macaques.** They could very easily steal them or, in the case of
chimps, dismember and eat them.

# The Most Dangerous Primate

Chimps are four times as strong as humans and arguably more
aggressive and violent. A recent study estimated that chimps
have twice the intraspecies (within their species) murder rate
of humans. The actual numbers are variable depending on the
group, but it's quite compelling regardless. Combined with
strong teeth and occasional rogue males, stringent safety
measures are recommended when humans and chimps live in
close proximity.

# How to Survive If a Gorilla Approaches

I outline here how to deal with a gorilla because groups of tourists occasionally go to see them. Aggressive encounters can generally be avoided if you follow a few recommended steps. If a gorilla approaches:

- **Show submission.**

- **Don't look them in the eye.**

- **Don't back away**—instead, stand your ground.

- **Don't run**—being still is your best bet.

- **Be calm** and pretend you're doing your own thing. Maybe you're just eating grass or looking at bugs. Whatever it is, this makes you look less intimidating.

- **Keep your fingers hidden.** Generally, if an ape or any monkey approaches or grabs you, it's best to keep your fingers protected because they love to bite fingers when they're fighting each other. I'm sure this is the first thing you'll be thinking about if a big ape grabs you.

**Fun Fact**

The pygmy mouse lemur of forests in eastern Madagascar is only two and a half inches long and is the smallest primate. It's definitely one you don't have to worry about.

# Crocodilians

I once had a girlfriend who had teeth-shaped scars across her chest. Those scars were from an unfortunate encounter with a crocodile while swimming beyond the "Beware of Crocodiles" sign! Everyone who heard what had happened wanted her to recount the story. It went something like this:

On a hot and muggy morning before the other tropical plant researchers got out of bed, she decided to go for a relaxing swim in the Panama Canal. There were signs that had recently been erected that said "Beware of Crocodiles," but because people had been swimming there for years, nobody paid attention to the signs.

The goal that day was to swim to a channel marker about a hundred meters offshore. At first, the swim was like any other. At seventy-five meters from shore, however, this dramatically changed. She remembers getting slammed in the chest and spun around. She had tooth marks across her chest and was staring at a massive crocodile. Its head and tail rose out of the water and it bellowed at her like a dragon awakened from its slumber. Then it sank beneath the surface, out of sight.

She screamed bloody murder, waking up the entire camp. I'm sure everyone assumed the worst, but thankfully the crocodile had disappeared and not done anything else. The crocodile researchers I've talked to think it was likely a territorial display, and the responding scream scared it as well. Either way, it was probably the best ending to a terrifying situation.

The visiting researchers at this site now pay attention to those signs, and nobody swims in the Panama Canal anymore! When I heard that story, it reinforced my already healthy fear of crocs.

DANGER
CROCODILES

NO
SWIMMING

I'll never forget the scene in *Crocodile Dundee* where a giant saltwater crocodile lunged out of the water to grab the American reporter sent to do an article on Mick Dundee in the Australian Outback. Luckily for her, the scene ends with Dundee killing what looks to be a fifteen-plus-foot crocodile. I saw that movie in high school, and I've been scared to death of going near any water in croc country ever since. But it so happens that, in my line of work, I very often find myself in croc country. In fact, I've conducted underwater research in the very croc-filled waters where my ex-girlfriend's incident took place. It's a living nightmare!

It was years after the incident, and I was helping a fish biologist put out gill nets to trap fish. The operation required us to snorkel down ten feet to install the nets in the croc-infested waters of the canal. Our basic understanding of the American crocodiles at the time was that we'd probably see them before they could attack. The idea was that an attack underwater was unlikely. So we came up with a plan. Five guards with guns stood around as we jumped into the water and did our little operation. I think at that stage I must have had a lot of trust that if I did have a run-in, they'd somehow shoot the croc instead of me. Fortunately there wasn't an incident, but it did make me think more about croc behavior and the dangers.

In the particular case of crocodiles, I think my fear is probably a good thing, because they are one of the very few animals that do actively hunt humans if given the opportunity. They really are what we'd refer to as man-eaters. This is not meant to vilify them—it's just a fact.

# The Basics

While there are twenty-five species of crocodilians, not all pose a serious threat to humans. Generally these reptiles have to be eight feet long or larger to be physically able to eat a person, and not all species get that large.

It's hard to tell exactly how many people a year are eaten by crocs because it's often in remote jungles and swamps that big crocs thrive. Many attacks are not reported to authorities, so the numbers are not exact. A few sources estimate that somewhere between three hundred and a thousand people a year are taken by crocodiles. Most of those are either the Nile crocodile or the saltwater crocodile. The mugger croc in India also accounts for a lot of deaths.

Besides those three, there are eight other dangerous crocodilians that have been known to take down and consume adult humans if given the chance.

1. West African crocodile
2. American crocodile
3. Morelet's crocodile
4. Orinoco crocodile
5. Cuban crocodile
6. Black caiman
7. Sunda gharial
8. American alligator

A few others have the ability to take small children or dogs: the freshwater crocodile, Philippine crocodile, Siamese crocodile, broad-snouted caiman, spectacled caiman, yacare caiman, and gharial.

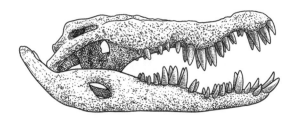

While many other organisms that exist today have changed significantly over time, crocodiles seem to have changed little in their evolution since the time of the dinosaurs. They first evolved around two hundred million years ago, and most species are still thriving today. In other words, they stumbled upon something that really worked—but what is that exactly?

Part of what makes crocs so dangerous is their ability to be sit-and-wait predators. They can literally be submerged underwater for about two hours without coming up for air—just waiting for prey to come by.

They also have the strongest known bite force of any large predator. Nile crocs have had recorded bites around 5,000 pounds per square inch. For perspective, the average human has a bite force around 162 pounds per square inch. If you get chomped by a croc, you won't be able to open their mouth. That's important to at least consider before getting yourself in a situation you can't get out of.

# Scenarios to Avoid

**Don't swim in waters known to have crocs.** This is a no-brainer, but if there is a sign that states they are around, it's likely there for a reason.

**Avoid swimming at dusk or night** in croc country—crocodiles often hunt at these times. Even if crocs aren't supposed to be present there, you should still swim with caution at these times.

**Don't get within fifteen feet of a crocodile,** as they're surprisingly fast at short range.

**Don't walk along the water's edge.** In fact, it's recommended to stay about fifteen feet from the edge of the water in croc country at all times.

**Avoid camping near water.** It's recommended that you set up camp no closer than fifty yards from the water in places where crocs live. Campers have gone missing when crocs have come out of the water and taken them from their camps. If you're wondering why I'm so afraid of crocodiles, it's because these facts are nightmare fuel for me.

**Don't get water from the same spot twice.** Crocs are clever in how they hunt. If they see someone gathering water at one spot on a waterway, they will move to that spot, submerge, and wait. This is also why I brought extra water when I'd camp in northern Australia.

**Avoid crocodile nests.** Like most mothers in the animal kingdom, they too are very aggressive when defending their offspring.

**Avoid feeding crocs.** Not only is it generally illegal and dangerous to give food to a crocodile in most places, it also teaches crocs to associate humans with food! That leads to more encounters, which will be bad for either the human or the croc, who will likely have to be put down.

# The Most Dangerous

While crocodiles over about eight feet pose a serious threat to humans, the Nile and saltwater crocs are the most dangerous of all species. Both of these actively hunt humans and will even crawl out of the water to take humans from the shore.

# How to Survive an Attack

Probably the best thing is to **stay alert and avoid getting attacked in the first place.** I can't emphasize this enough. You do not want to deal with a croc when you're in their mouth. That's because once a croc clamps down on you, it's basically impossible to open its jaws. However, if you do find yourself in this situation, I suppose you should have a plan. Here's a hot tip: crocs do have sensitive spots—their eyes, nostrils, and throat.

**Poke it in the eyes.** If you can have the wherewithal to get your fingers or something else into these sensitive organs, the croc may release you.

If the eyes are unreachable, the next most vulnerable areas are the **nostrils and throat.** Crocodiles have a flap of skin that keeps water out of their throats. If your hand is caught inside a croc's mouth, you may be able to pull this flap down and it could release you.

**Don't assume it'll let you go.** A misconception is that maybe you can "play dead" and it'll think you've drowned and release you. Nobody will be able to hold their breath that long. Fight.

**Get out of the water** as soon as you're released and run to safety.

**Get medical attention right away.** Even small puncture wounds could get infected easily because of the multitudes of bacteria in their mouths and the waters they live in.

# The Take-Home

I'm sure that your takeaway from this chapter is a healthy respect or fear of crocodilians. From a safety standpoint, that is by far the best way to view them. At the same time, they are amazing creatures in their own right.

Crocodiles are apex predators in their ecosystems. That's biologist talk for: "They're important for a balanced natural system." I would never advocate for their complete removal from an ecosystem. They play valuable ecological roles in the areas where they live.

I would also argue that having these massive man-eaters around is good for your own psyche, if nothing else than to remind us that we're not always the top dog everywhere. It's a good grounding, I suppose.

And, for goodness' sake, if there are any signs that say "Beware of Crocodiles," give the sign installers the benefit of the doubt and don't go for a swim!

# Wild Boar

I'll never forget the 1957 Walt Disney classic *Old Yeller,* a movie about a boy and his faithful dog. At the climax of the film, the dog bravely defends the young boy from being attacked by a pack of wild hogs. The dog's boldness creates just enough of a distraction for the boy to get away up a tree, but Old Yeller is wounded. Later, the dog defends him from a rabid wolf and contracts rabies from it. Ultimately this leads to the tragic scene of his death—still one of the saddest movie scenes ever. The pigs were villains in this story and, I would guess, countless other stories throughout history!

So that raises the question: How can we make sure we don't suffer the same fate and avoid encounters with wild boar?

# The Basics

The ferocity of wild pigs is legendary. It's even been the subject of cave paintings going back at least 15,000 years. This is a cave painting re-creation in the style of those found in Spain during that time.

Globally there are eight living pig species. I'm talking here mainly about wild boar, aka feral hogs. This is a term used to describe the wild version of our domesticated pigs.

People don't generally think of those little pink pigs you see in children's cartoons as ferocious. This couldn't be further from the truth. If released from the farm, they quickly drift back into a wilder version—what we commonly call the feral hog. Make no mistake, these animals can get large and powerful, and can be very dangerous.

One of the largest wild hogs ever was reported to weigh 1,000 pounds and be 12 feet long. The pig was named Hogzilla and became a viral sensation in 2004. After exhuming the corpse for a *National Geographic* episode, scientist John Mayer determined it was closer to 800 pounds and 8.5 feet long.

In 2007, another viral pig surfaced. "Monster Pig," as it was named, was killed in Alabama by an eleven-year-old boy. It weighed 1,050 pounds and measured 9 feet 4 inches.

Unfortunately, it seems like the story was only partly true, as the animal turned out to be a formerly domestic pig that had gone feral and was living on a private commercial hunting preserve. Either way, these two reports show how large these pigs can get.

Pigs also eat almost anything. Technically they are omnivores. People know they'll eat kitchen scraps, but they'll also eat meat. They'll eat grain, grubs, tasty plant roots, carrion, and even their caretakers if given the opportunity. For me, this doesn't make them man-eaters, but it's a reminder not to "play dead" around a pig.

Attacks by wild hogs are rare, but they occur more often than attacks by large predators, like wolves. One study analyzed 412 documented attacks from 1825 to 2012 that involved 665 people. Seventy percent of those attacks were in the last twelve years of the study—which means the attacks are increasing.

# Other Big Pigs

While we're on the topic of pigs, let's not forget that there are other wild pigs that have walked and are walking planet earth. Here are a few from our past and present.

**The "Hell Pig" or entelodont** was a famous pig-like ancestor that was close to living pigs on the evolutionary tree. It thrived for about thirty million years, from about fifty million years ago (abbreviated mya) up to about nineteen mya. It is estimated that they could reach about 2,000 pounds and were massive predators on the plains of North America and Eurasia.

**Warthogs,** like the cartoon warthog Pumbaa in the *Lion King*, roam the African savanna and can weigh up to 165 pounds.

**Giant forest hogs** live in central Africa and can reach over 600 pounds.

**Bush pigs**, also African, can weigh 330 pounds.

The **red river hog**, another African pig, has a beautiful red coat and can grow to about 250 pounds.

**Babirusas** are pigs found in and around Sulawesi and sport massive canine tusks, giving them a super prehistoric

look. In fact, the upper canines grow up and out of the skull on the top. These pigs can reach 220 pounds.

 **Peccaries**, while not technically in the pig family, are the closest thing the New World has to native pigs. In total there are three species, and the largest of them don't even get to 100 pounds.

# Scenarios to Avoid

Wild boar are aggressive. When they attack, the injuries are mostly lacerations and punctures. In severe cases, this could lead to fatality due to blood loss. Basically, you'll want to avoid getting attacked. Here are a few recommendations to stay safe.

- **Avoid traveling alone** on foot in rural areas, especially in areas with dense thickets.

- **Walking with a dog could provoke an attack** if you come across a wild boar, so be mindful of this.

- **Don't threaten or chase a pig** out of an agricultural field or garden.

- **Don't approach an injured pig.** In a wounded state, they're likely to lash out in self-defense.

- **Don't try to feed or pet a wild pig**. This not only associates humans with food, but could lead to habituation and loss of fear of humans. It can also result in you getting either bitten or injured.

- **Don't block the path of a fleeing pig.**

# The Most Dangerous

**Solitary large males** are the largest and most aggressive individuals you could encounter. Even worse is **a big, angry, injured animal**. Occasionally you might find **a group of pigs** that proves to be a threat as well.

Technically, about twice as many attacks happen in the winter months as in the summer, but you could be attacked at any time.

# How to Survive a Wild Hog Attack

Playing dead in a pig attack is a bad approach, mainly because it gives the pig the opportunity to gore your stomach—which is bad. So, here are a few tried-and-true methods that have worked for survivors of pig attacks.

- First, if you see a pig approaching from a distance, **run away.** Keep in mind that they're fast, so this won't work if they're already very close.

- If they continue approaching you, try to **get up a tree.** They can't climb, so six feet up and you're probably safe.

- If there are no trees around, stand your ground and prepare to **fight the pig.** If you don't have a gun, knife, or spear, use anything you have. This might include a tripod, bike, shovel, or dog leash. Try your best and never give up.

- **Stay on your feet.** If you fall, you risk getting a tusk in the gut, arms, head, or neck.

- **Keep fighting** until the pig stops. Often attacks only last a minute.

- **Get first aid immediately.** Not only do you need to prevent blood loss, but pigs also carry a lot of harmful bacteria in their mouths that could cause serious problems if untreated.

# Rhinos

Rhinos are generally gentle and keep to themselves, but they are definitely not pacifists. If they are threatened, they'll move their bodies into an attack stance and often charge in an attempt to get rid of the perceived threat. To understand what to do, however, it's important to look at their physiology and what behaviors may indicate their intent to attack.

## The Basics

First, rhinos are the largest land mammals after the African and Asian elephants. Their massive, muscled bodies have both thick skin and big horns to protect them from predators on the grasslands. Possibly as a consequence of having these remarkable ways of protecting themselves, which deter most would-be predators, they don't have or need great eyesight.

In studies of rhino eyes, it seems that a rhino has a hard time distinguishing individual humans from only thirty feet away. Beyond a hundred meters, it's almost impossible for them to recognize a human silhouette. Their eyesight is considered one of the worst in the animal kingdom—up there with bats and moles.

What they lack in eyesight, they seem to make up for with keen auditory (hearing) and olfactory (smell) senses. In fact, the largest part of a rhino brain is dedicated to the sense of smell. This has big implications for how we treat them and how we can stay safe near them.

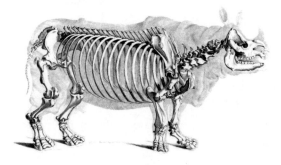

# Scenarios to Avoid

- 🔥 **Don't surprise a rhino.** Their first instinct is to charge a threat, whether or not it is actually a threat.

- 🔥 **Don't mess with a mother or baby rhino.** They're very protective of their young and will fend off threats.

- 🔥 **Approaching a rhino is never a good idea**, and it's an even worse idea in an open habitat with no clear place to hide.

# The Most Dangerous

**Black rhinos** are known to be much more aggressive than the other rhino species. White rhinos, however, because they are about four times as numerous, have had more human deaths associated with them.

# How to Survive an Attack

If for some reason you've not taken the best advice—which is to never approach a rhino—and you're now face-to-face with the fourth largest land animal on earth, let's walk through a few ways to try to stay alive.

1. **Stay fairly still.** Remember, rhinos can't see well, so if you're fairly still and don't seem to be a threat, they may mistake you for a tree and keep grazing.

2. **Stay downwind of the rhino.** Like other animals, they sense you mainly via smell. If you're downwind, they can't smell you.

3. **Climb a tree** if there is one nearby. They can't climb, and if you can get up a few feet they're probably not going to pursue. If you can't get up the tree, standing behind it is a good approach.

4. **Run for the scrub** if that's the only option. Sometimes it's dry and desert-like in Africa, but there are spiny shrubs all over. It's rare that the rhino will pursue you into these bushes. A few cuts from thorns is better than being gored to death, right? Right.

5. **Run for a rock or vehicle** if that's possible. Rhinos can tip over vehicles, but you're much better off inside than exposed.

6. **Shouting and yelling** might work to stop an attack if there is no option of cover. Make sounds that are unfamiliar to a rhino. This includes singing, shouting, and clapping. This is a great reason to have your favorite song in mind when you are adventuring in Africa.

7. **Running in a zigzag pattern** is recommended. You can definitely turn faster than a rhino. If the rhino misses while it is chasing you one way, turn and **run in the opposite direction**. They rarely continue an attack in the opposite direction.

8. **Distract the rhino with a bag or shirt**—If the charge is imminent and you can't find anything to hide behind, know that right before contact, the rhino will put its head down. At this stage you might be able to throw a

backpack, shirt, or other object up to distract the rhino and get to safety.

### Fun Rhino Facts

The horn of a white rhino can be as long as sixty-two inches!

Rhino horn, despite the rumor, does nothing medically. Yet, because of this superstition, rhino horn is worth more than its weight in gold. This has given rise to poachers, who have driven populations to near extinction.

The extinct rhino *Paraceratherium* was one of the largest mammals to have walked the earth. It stood sixteen feet at the shoulder and weighed over twenty tons. That's a good 50 percent larger than modern elephants.

# Poison Ivy

*"The poisoned weed is much in shape like our English Ivy, but being but touched, causeth rednesse, itching, and lastly blisters."*

—Explorer John Smith, 1624

I can only imagine that, sometime before 1966, comic book writer Robert Kanigher of *Batman* fame must have had a bad encounter with poison ivy and then come up with the antiheroine Poison Ivy. Then again, maybe he only heard that poison ivy can kill you and thought it was a cool name—who knows! What's unusual is that poison ivy doesn't contain a toxin, and it kills in a way that's contrary to almost everything we know about toxins in plants.

# The Basics

It turns out that poison ivy is deadly because of an oil within the plant called urushiol. This oil isn't a toxin. It's a relatively harmless compound, except for the fact that most people's bodies have an adverse reaction to it.

A good analogy here is allergies to tree pollen or house cats. Petting a cat is pretty harmless, unless you happen to be allergic to cats. If you are allergic to the felines, your body overreacts to what it thinks is a threat—and you break out in rashes, itching, and, in the worst-case scenario, anaphylaxis (which can hinder your ability to breathe and can send the body into shock).

Urushiol is somewhat similar in that it's more of an allergen. The first time someone gets urushiol oil from poison ivy on their skin, they may not react at all. The body has never encountered the compound and doesn't have antibodies to mount a defense. It may take a week or more for your body to produce enough antibodies for a rash or other reaction to occur. The initial response to the plant's oils can be delayed, but when you have had enough exposure to build antibodies, you get a quicker reaction each time you're exposed after that.

Classic reactions to poison ivy involve puss-filled red rashes that itch like crazy. Often it creates large blisters. Scratching them breaks the skin and oozing puss goes all over. One positive thing is that the oozing liquid is not toxic, and it won't spread anything. It's just gross. If you've ever had this happen to you, you won't soon forget.

# How to Identify Poison Ivy

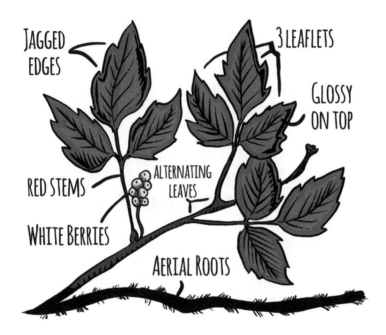

JAGGED EDGES

3 LEAFLETS

GLOSSY ON TOP

RED STEMS

ALTERNATING LEAVES

WHITE BERRIES

AERIAL ROOTS

Identifying the plant is important. It's your first defense. There are three easy-to-remember phrases that are often used to identify poison ivy.

1. **"Leaves of three, let it be."** Granted, there are some other things in the forest with leaves in clusters of three—like box elder, kudzu, and blackberries—but this phrase is a good start.

2. **"Hairy vine, no friend of mine."** Many vines only have leaves far up in the canopy. That means all you'd see is a vine attached to a tree. Yet poison ivy has a very characteristic "hairy" vine. If you touched that hairy vine, you'd also get exposed to the dangerous oils.

3.  **"Berries of white, danger in sight."** Many of the berries you'll see in the forest are red, so a small white berry is, at the very least, a caution to look out for poison ivy. Just realize that berries are only present on the plant for a short period of time.

If you're still uncertain, you can (of course) do a quick internet search on your phone to make sure you're correctly identifying poison ivy. Once you correctly identify it, it will become easy to spot! I have a fun, detailed video on this via *StoneAgeMan* on YouTube.

# Scenarios to Avoid

- **Don't burn poison ivy.** The smoke will get into your lungs and coat them with the oils. It will also cover your clothes and skin with a fine layer of oil. This can be disastrous. I've seen the fallout from burning poison ivy firsthand when my best friend was covered in smoke from a nearby prescribed burn in the forest. His entire torso and legs were covered in pus-filled boils, and it took lots of medication and time to fully recover.

- **Don't eat the berries.** Your throat, which you definitely need for breathing properly, could swell and react adversely.

- **Be careful petting your dog** in poison ivy country. Dogs rarely react to poison ivy, but the oil can stay on their fur and transfer it to anyone who touches them.

- 🔥 **Don't skin a rabbit** that's been living in poison ivy and then wear the pelt on your body without first washing it thoroughly. Let's just say I know someone who figured this out the hard way. Those oils are persistent and hard to get off.

# The Most Dangerous

The most dangerous poison ivy seems to be the kind you can't see. In the winter, it is common to grab sticks and dead vines to burn in a campfire, some of which may actually be leafless poison ivy. Two of my colleagues have had severe poison ivy reactions from inhaling smoke in this fashion. Both went to the emergency room because their whole body swelled up from the reaction.

# How to Survive Poison Ivy Rashes and Get Better

The biggest key to surviving and preventing a reaction is being able to identify poison ivy and making sure you **wash the oils away properly.** I get exposed to a lot in the forests of the Carolinas, but properly washing up goes a long way to prevent a rash.

If you can already identify poison ivy, you'll know when you were exposed. The next step is to wash within two to eight hours of getting any part of this plant in contact with your skin. In addition to washing your skin, wash anything that came into contact with the plants—boots, pants, shovels, gloves, etc. The oil will stay on these and cause reactions even a year later!

If, for some reason, you didn't wash it off and you start reacting, know that it'll be bad for a few days, and then it may take a month or more to fully recover. Calamine lotion, cortisone, and Benadryl are often what you'll use as topical treatments to alleviate the symptoms.

Whatever you do, try not to scratch away at the rash and blisters. Doing so could cause bacteria to invade, resulting in a severe infection.

If it gets worse, a dermatologist may prescribe something stronger, like a steroid called prednisone to reduce the inflammation and mask the painful symptoms. If you are having a severe reaction, a dermatologist is your new best friend.

## Fun Fact

Urushiol and related oils are found in other plants and can cause similar reactions from them. Plants like poison oak and poison sumac are very similar. Most people may know that. However, related plants in the Anacardiaceae family, like cashews and mangoes, can cause reactions in susceptible people as well. My wife loves mangoes. On our honeymoon, we sat in a mango grove and gorged ourselves silly with perfectly ripe fruits, juicy goodness dripping from our faces and hands. Unfortunately, that was also the day we found out she was allergic to mango skin—Haley's face and neck broke out in a mask of red itchiness. We still love to eat mango—we just avoid the skin like it's poison ivy now!

# Edible and Deadly Plants

If you love Harry Potter and long to take Herbology or Potions Class so you can learn the mystery and magic of plants in the world, you're in luck! Plants are amazing, and learning to identify and use them in traditional ways (even some in your own backyard) is about as close to real magic as it gets in the muggle world! At their most fundamental, plants can provide shelter, food, oxygen, and warmth. Plants can also contain deadly poisons and cures for a myriad of maladies. The forest is a natural medicine cabinet, and using this diverse resource the right way can certainly make you feel like you're at Hogwarts concocting healing potions! There are so many things you can do with plants, if only you know what you're looking at. That's why plants are essential to basic wilderness survival. Even though this is a broad crash course in some great plants to know, I hope you get a sense of how important they are to all of us. And with a little research, I bet you'll find the natural history and uses of real plants to be just as fascinating as fictional ones. Even though mandrake root is not actually a live

humanoid baby with a scream that can render you unconscious, *real* mandrake has hallucinogenic properties reportedly used in rituals dating back to Norse paganism!

Let's start with poisonous plants. Here are some basic guidelines to keep from dying from a poisonous plant.

# How Not to Become a Plant-Induced Corpse

1. **Learn as much as you can.** That's why you're reading this book. This is the first step. Learn which plants you can eat, and which are deadly.

2. **Never eat plants you don't know**. Surely someone in history came upon an unknown plant and tasted it. If they died, we learned not to eat it. Today, all that hard work

is done. You can learn to correctly identify plants with guides and many other resources (like taking one of our wilderness survival courses) before you just go popping it in your mouth.

3. **Cover your skin.** Many plants cause some irritation if touched. Poison ivy or stinging nettles won't be as much of a problem if you're wearing pants and long sleeves.

4. **Wash your hands.** Believe it or not, if you wash your hands after touching a toxic plant, you'll probably be fine! The skin on your fingers is tough. Touching your eyes or nose, or eating the plant afterward, is the real danger.

5. **Touch pets with care.** A dog or a rabbit can run through poison ivy and not have a problem. You can actually get it from them just by petting their oily fur.

6. **Make fire with known plants**. Since some plants are toxic because of the chemicals inside them, burning them will consequently release some really terrible compounds into the air. You don't want to breathe in that smoke!

# Edible/Useful Plants

I am a huge fan of eating wild edibles. In fact, I want to start with some of those after we've established some ground rules:

1. **Don't eat something you haven't certainly identified**. Many plants look similar, so you want to make sure you use every possible resource to correctly identify a plant. Going out to learn plants with a guide or taking a wilderness course is the safest way to begin.

2. **Avoid eating any plants growing in places with pesticides or possible contamination**, like railroad

tracks, golf courses, public areas with lots of traffic, and along roadways.

3. **Try edibles at first in small amounts**. This makes sure you don't react poorly to something. Even if something is not poisonous, it still may not agree with you, so starting small is the smart way to go.

4. **Don't mix a lot of plants together** until you're familiar with them.

I'll start first with a few of the many plants that you can eat. Knowing these is actually important for survival situations, as you can forage and survive with just this little bit of wilderness knowledge. It's also a fun way to look at the world and discover there are many things to eat right nearby!

**Dandelions:** Most people wouldn't think you can eat dandelions, but they are definitely edible. They are one of the easiest to identify as well. The flowers are really tasty and good for obtaining vitamin D.

**Currants:** Currants have a lot of wonderful vitamin C. They're tasty and somewhat tart at times.

**Wild onions,** just like our domesticated onions, can be harvested and added as amendments to your dishes.

**Alfalfa:** Alfalfa seeds and dried leaves can be taken as a supplement for their nutritional qualities. The seeds can be sprouted and eaten in the form of alfalfa sprouts.

**Violets:** Violet flowers contain large amounts of vitamin C. The leaves are also high in vitamin A. They make a colorful and tasty addition to salads.

**Grass:** All grasses are edible, but some are tastier than others. The woody bits are somewhat difficult to digest, so it's best to find the most tender parts of the grass or simply more tender types of grass, like ryegrass.

**Salsify:** This is closely related to dandelions, but is not bitter like dandelions. You can harvest the flower buds, growing meristems and edible roots. There is white sap in the plant that is also perfectly okay to eat.

**Wild mustards:** Mustards are extremely nutritious and add a lot of spice to meals. All mustard plants smell like mustard, so this is one easy way to identify them beyond their morphology.

**Shepherd's purse:** The entire plant is edible, but the seed pods are the distinguishing feature. They look like small hearts.

**Pineapple weed:** Also known as wild chamomile, it is completely edible. The best way to identify pineapple weed is via the smell. It smells a lot like pineapple.

**Lamb's quarters:** It looks much like quinoa and tastes like spinach. It grows as a weed all over the world and contains a lot of calcium. The smallest leaves are the most nutritious.

**Green amaranth:** This plant has a big spiky seed pod on the top. You wouldn't eat the seed pods, though. You would, instead, eat the smooth stems and leaves.

**Common mallow:** This is a plant related to okra. The disk-shaped leaves are tasty. The disk-shaped button fruits are also really delicious. You can boil it and use it in gumbos, just like okra.

**Purslane:** The entire plant is edible. This is the number one wild edible for omega-3 fatty acids. It can be found almost anywhere, sprawling low along the ground.

**Roses:** All roses are edible, and people love to grow roses. They are rich in iron. Leaves can be used in salads (so long as you haven't put pesticides on them). The petals, buds, and rose hips are also edible.

**Miner's lettuce:** It's the romaine lettuce of the wild edible world. The big heart-shaped leaves are great for salads.

# Deadly Plants

**Knowing the dangerous and deadly plants is important.** If you at least know the deadly ones first, then you can have some confidence that you can experiment a bit with others I listed above. Just remember that—if you're unsure or new to all this—don't do it alone. I highly recommend you find someone with more knowledge of plants to teach you. There are some great wilderness courses out there that have an edible plant component if you want some hands-on experience with experts. I have taken groups like this out all over the world, as I do now via StoneAgeMan.com.

**Poison hemlock:** The Greek philosopher Socrates is said to have died by drinking a concoction made with poison hemlock.

**Death camas:** Resembling wild onion in its early leaves, death camas contains the alkaloid zygacine—which if consumed is potentially lethal to humans.

**Monkshood:** This is one of the deadliest plants in existence. It's also called wolfsbane and was often used in the homesteading days to poison wolves by adding it to the meat of dead animals.

**Oleander:** Death from this plant is somewhat rare, yet many legends exist about it. One legend has it that cooking a hot dog on an oleander stick will kill you. That's not true. But, sadly, there are accounts of small children who have died from eating leaves off oleander hedges.

 **Poison ivy, Poison oak, Poison sumac:** Even though we spent an entire chapter on poison ivy, it's worth a reminder here that there are plants that contain oily resins that can cause terrible allergic reactions. The more exposure you have to these plants, the quicker your body gets an immune response, meaning you react more with more exposures.

 **Angel's trumpet:** Many homes in the tropical south have this beautiful flower growing outside in the yard, yet eating a flower is enough to send you into terrible hallucinations and even kill you.

**Foxglove:** Also known as dead man's bells or witch's gloves, this beautiful ornamental plant contains a host of toxic glycosides. One is digoxin, a powerful drug that can stop your heart. Taken in small doses, though, it is used to treat patients with congestive heart failure.

 **Jimsonweed:** While this is a hallucinogenic plant that has been used in traditional medicine for millennia, the likelihood of an overdose is high. It contains dangerous levels of atropine, hyoscyamine, and scopolamine.

 **White snakeroot:** People can die simply by drinking the milk of animals that eat this plant. In fact, it killed Abraham Lincoln's mother—who, coincidentally, is one of my ancestors!

 **Deadly nightshade:** It looks a bit like blueberries or small tomatoes. It contains atropine and solanine.

 **Hellebore:** While a common yard plant for gardeners, it's also somewhat toxic. A new theory suggests this may have been the plant that killed Alexander the Great.

# Other Deadly Plants

 There really are a lot of plants that are deadly or toxic to some degree. I mean, plants are just sitting there, and without some sort of toxin to deter would-be grazers, how would they survive?

These are a few others to be aware of and look up for their deadly toxic characteristics. Plus, I think some of their names are just terrific!

Belladonna, castor bean, dumb cane,
manchineel tree, rosary pea, pokeweed,
mountain laurel, white baneberry, corn cockle,
larkspur, wild poinsettia, jack-in-the-pulpit, iris,
daffodil, elderberry (uncooked), stinging nettle,
giant hogweed, wild parsnip.

# Deadly Mushrooms

Unlike the more sensational animals, like bears, crocodiles, and sharks (that have entire weeks devoted to them in the media), there are far fewer documentaries about the wonderful world of mushrooms. Maybe that's why they're so intriguing to me, like little undiscovered gems in the forest. Most people are aware that they exist but know almost nothing about their hidden lives. It's difficult for people to identify even a few common mushrooms in the forest. That changed for Haley and me one summer when we went on a quest to look for and film some of the world's deadliest mushrooms.

In our journey to understand the deadly mushrooms, we met up with a few really interesting mycologists—the real mushroom professionals. Every mycologist we met was overly excited about helping us find those deadly ones, but also wanted to fill us with mind-boggling facts about the edible ones they were either growing or picking wild. Stuff like:

- The largest and oldest organism on the planet is a honey mushroom. It covers 3.7 million square meters in Oregon and is estimated to be 8,650 years old.

- There are 14,000 described species of mushrooms.

- Much as in *Avatar,* where everything is connected in the forest, fungal mycelium in forests acts kind of like a neurological network in nature.

- Reindeer love to eat psychoactive mushrooms in the Arctic north, which may be how they "fly" at Christmas (more on that later).

With these new facts in mind, we set off to try our own hand at growing these hidden gems. That summer, a massive oak branch fell in our backyard, so we decided to use that recently fallen piece of wood to grow some edible shiitakes. We drilled a hundred holes in that branch and seeded them with some purchased mushroom spawn. Over the course of the next three years, we watched several "flushes" of big, edible, and quite delicious mushrooms emerge. Because I inoculated this log, I always knew they were edible. As for foraging wild mushrooms, it took years before I gained enough experience to trust myself enough to identify and eat an edible mushroom I had not seeded myself.

This isn't a guide to show you how to hunt and eat mushrooms in the wild, though it's a common practice enjoyed in many places the world over. This guide is here to point out a few of the dangers that might exist with wild mushrooms. If you eat the wrong one, there are some very real consequences. This will become clear as I describe one of the most recognizable of them all. Even if you have never heard of it, I know you would recognize it—the red-and-white fly agaric.

## The Fly Agaric

*Amanita muscaria* is commonly known as the fly agaric because it was used to collect and kill flies. It's a big mushroom that has a reddish cap with white flecks. You've probably seen it in drawings even if you had no idea what it was called. If you've played Mario Brothers or watched the Smurfs, you've seen it. It's that red-and-white spotted mushroom that helps Mario grow bigger, no doubt a nod to the hallucinogenic properties of this mushroom. The Smurfs live in Smurftastic houses that happen to be those very same Amanita mushrooms.

It's one of the most influential mushrooms among all of mankind. Some have even considered it the original soma, an inspiration for the Hindu religion. Others have suggested that the red-and-white outfit that modern-day Santa Claus wears and the stories of flying reindeer all stem back to rituals with this mushroom in Nordic countries.

But this isn't the kind of mushroom you want to eat. In fact, if you eat a dozen or more of them, it'll likely kill you. That's a lot to eat in one sitting, and the repercussions are not ideal. You may experience hallucinations, nausea, vomiting, and dizziness, and even have a seizure. Fortunately, you can recover fully afterwards, if you don't die. That's not true for some of the others in our list.

**The death cap,** for instance, looks similar to the fly agaric—distinguished only by color to the untrained eye. This yellow to white mushroom is responsible for half of the deaths from mushroom poisonings. It's believed to have killed the Roman Emperor Claudius in AD 54 and the Emperor Charles VI in 1740. One single cap has enough toxin to kill two adults.

One of the big problems with death caps is that they taste and look really pleasant. That's a bad combination if your method of foraging in the forest includes randomly picking mushrooms and popping them in your mouth. Add to that the fact that the symptoms are delayed, and you have a deadly recipe.

At first, you may just have an upset stomach, feel nauseous, and vomit a few times. A couple of days later this will probably go away, so you might think you're in the clear—but that's when the more serious complications can occur. The liver is being destroyed, and kidney failure is also likely. Death generally occurs six to sixteen days after poisoning.

In 2012, four people were accidentally poisoned by the death caps when they were served at a New Year's dinner party in Canberra, Australia. Everyone was rushed to the hospital. Two died and one had to have a liver transplant.

And these aren't the only mushrooms that can kill you. There are mushrooms called webcaps, skullcaps, destroying angels, and deadly dapperlings that can kill you, too. Even so, I don't want you to fear mushrooms—just be smart. So I've come up with a few best practices to start you on your way.

# Mushroom Best Practices

- **Don't eat any mushroom you can't identify.** This is the first and most important rule.

- **Don't trust size and color when you identify mushrooms.** Unlike plants and animals, mushrooms vary widely in size and color, and identification is often made using more subtle characteristics.

- **Learn first all of the deadly or toxic mushrooms** so that you make sure you're not ingesting one that will kill you quickly.

- **Go on mushroom hikes with professionals** or mushroom collectors you trust to help you identify mushrooms. There are incredible mushroom clubs you can be a part of, and the hands-on experience you gain with them will probably be the most valuable. I highly suggest joining a club.

- **Start reading and learning about mushrooms.** There are lots of great books, and this is a great way to start.

- **Experiment with eating mushrooms from the grocery store first**. This is just a safe way to begin your edible forays. Mushrooms have tremendous health benefits, and you can start without fear of getting poisoned.

Don't forget that mushrooms are also amazing! Get a book and start looking for them on your next hike. Just don't randomly pop wild mushrooms in your mouth until you're a seasoned pro!

# More Animals

I need to be very clear that there are a lot of animals, plants, fungi, and parasites that I missed. I can't cover them all in one book, but I had to at least mention the following:

**Cone snails** are a small group of marine predatory snails that hunt with the help of a small harpoon-shaped radula tooth. They are brightly colored and often attractive to collectors. Don't collect them, though, as they could be deadly once in your pocket. Cone snails have been the cause of twenty-seven human deaths!

**Octopus and squid** are cephalopods. Jules Verne's *Captain Nemo* is about a fight against giant octopuses and, while it's fiction, make no mistake, cephalopods are large and have some inherent dangers associated with that. The largest squid, the colossal squid, is thought to reach thirty-three feet long! You don't want that animal wrapping a tentacle around you. Also of note, all octopedes have venom, but few are fatally dangerous. The famously dangerous blue-ringed octopus has enough venom to kill ten adult humans!

**African buffalos** are known sometimes as "the Black Death" or "the widowmakers" and probably deserved a chapter of their own given that they're credited with killing upwards of two hundred people a year. This is usually via goring from their horns. In fact, one study noted that they killed the person 49.5 percent of the time there was an "attack." Treat these like bison on steroids. Keep your distance. They basically use an "attack is our best defense" strategy. That makes them especially dangerous.

**Seals and sea lions** are pinnipeds. They're both predators and prey, so they fit into a unique category in our animal list. Generally, they're just curious and not a problem, but don't forget that they're large and have big canine teeth. Southern elephant seals, for instance, can weigh seven thousand pounds and can be very territorial on their beaches. The best advice is to be very cautious and back away if surrounded by pinnipeds.

**Hyenas** are large carnivores in Africa. In total, there are four species, but they're somewhat similar in behavior. Some scavenge more than they hunt, but they all have massive, powerful jaws. The largest are capable of killing an adult human and have been known to attack people when food is scarce. Best to treat them like lions. Stay in the car when you're in the bush. It's a dangerous place.

 **The big cats,** like lions, tigers, jaguars, leopards, and mountain lions are all really different in their behaviors. I plan on doing an extensive review of all of these in a future book so I can give each their due diligence. But be wary of hiking alone, letting little kids out of your sight, or turning your back on any of them. They'll seize the opportunity to make you prey. Farmers in tiger country, for instance, often wear a backward-facing mask to prevent tigers from sneaking up on them. Mountain lions in North America are responsible for a few attacks, but those are actually quite uncommon.

 **Komodo dragons** are the largest monitor lizards and are found on the island of Komodo. If you're on that island, the chances are high that you'll get a debrief on what to do, but let this be your first warning. They can weigh upwards of 150 pounds and have massively powerful jaws. Komodo dragons actually have a mildly venomous bite, too. In Komodo National Park, between 1974 and 2012, they were responsible for twenty-four human attacks, five of which were fatal. Basically, give them space, and if you do get bitten, seek medical attention quickly to prevent infection.

 **Spiders** could probably fill a book of their own. But the way I see it is that they're small and really want nothing to do with you. Their venom is meant for the prey

they eat and, yes, they could bite you. Some are pretty venomous, too. Most bites, however, are only because they feel threatened. So if you don't step on them or stick your foot in a boot with them in it, you'll probably be fine. With spiders, you just have to let them have their space and you're good.

 **Ants and wasps** both belong to the hymenopteran order of insects. They can bite and sting— sometimes to very painful ends. But they're rarely deadly, unless you're allergic. The most painful stings are from bullet ants, tarantula hawks, and warrior wasps. Who determined that, you might ask? It's all part of the Schmidt Pain Index, a scale developed by none other than an adventurous entomologist who thought it'd be a good idea to get stung by as many insects as he could—for science.

# How to Treat an Animal Not Listed

My hope is that you've learned a bit about what to do with some of these other animals and can draw a logical conclusion about others. If you can guess at how it lives in its environment, here are a few generalized recommendations of what to do:

1.  **Is it a prey animal?** If so, it may fight back defensively. Your best bet is probably to get out of its space quickly. That might mean running or slowly backing away. You'll have to make that call on the fly.

2.  **Is it colorful?** Many small invertebrates, snakes, and fish are brightly colored. This is often a signal for predators to stay away because they pack a punch. While there are lots of animals that mimic these colors, you can always play it safe and leave them alone. Definitely don't eat them. More simply, I don't recommend messing with colorful critters.

3.  **Is it a predator?** If so, what do you think its relationship is with humans? If you're in North or South America, it may not see you as potential prey. But if you mimic their natural prey, it may trigger them to treat you like prey. You're better off having them mistake you for a fellow predator. That's why getting big and yelling are good techniques. If you are someplace where humans may have been on the menu (think tiger, lion, or crocodile), you better be careful. Avoid letting them see you as food, and give them a lot of space. Having some safe space for yourself nearby is always a good idea.

Remember, most animals and plants are *not* trying to kill you. I highlighted a bunch in this book that might be considered man-eaters, but those really are rare. Every one of them, though, is just trying to survive in their ecosystem. They've been adapting to their particular habitat for millennia.

My goal for this wildlife survival guide was just to give you a better appreciation for how these animals might view the world. How might they see you? How can you avoid getting killed, while also appreciating how they're adapted to their ecosystem? The rest of this book is a bit more like a reference for bushcraft that might be useful to have in the back of your head as you wander into the great outdoors.

May your journey be memorable, and may you come back in one piece!

# PART II:

# Your Basic
# Survival Guide

# A Crash Course in How to Survive

You have one mission here, and that's to **never stop exploring** this wonderful thing we call nature. Not only could your survival be dependent on that, but through the knowledge you gain here, you may be able to make sure that some of the myths and rumors that come with the animals, plants, and situations that we're discussing here are set straight.

# Your Basic Kit

Your kit doesn't have to be elaborate. In fact, I always try to emphasize that you don't need much to get out and start exploring. However, I would recommend you bring these basic things when you go tromping off the grid.

**A cutting tool:** It could be as simple as a razor blade or as complex as a Swiss army knife, complete with saws, scissors, and screwdrivers. However, here I'll be recommending the ultimate bushcrafter's tool, a fixed-blade knife (that means you don't fold it up). It'll help you cut wood if you wish, whittle a spear, or cut your apple. I'll go into more detail on blades in the next section!

**Shelter:** Remember that old saying that you only need food, water, and shelter to survive? Well, if you're not building your shelter every night, I'd recommend taking a shelter with you. That could be a tent with sleeping bags and a rainfly. It could also be simpler—maybe a tarp and a hammock. Whatever it is, you need to spend a bit of time thinking about what you're going to do at night to stay dry and warm. Without a good night's sleep, you're not going to enjoy the rest of your exploring.

**Rope**: People in the industry usually refer to this category as your cordage, but just saying "rope" works too. You need this! In a pinch, you can use it to make your own shelter, make a trap, or lower yourself off a cliff. You don't have to start by bringing a hundred yards of high-strength rappelling cord. Most of the time, you just need some as backup in case of emergencies. I recommend at least having paracord. It's a military-grade cord and it's the stuff people make those survival bracelets out of. You can store it in your bag or wear it via a bracelet on your arm. I'll go into the important knots to learn with your rope (cordage) in a few chapters.

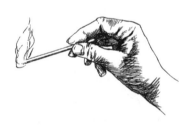

**Fire-starter:** Much like your rope, a fire-starter is in case you get into a pinch. I like to have a lighter and a set of waterproof matches in the bag. But you might also want to have a small piece of flint and steel that you can create sparks with. It takes some practice to light a fire with this technique, but if you do get stuck, you'll have a lot of time to practice! Actually, that's probably a bad time to figure it out. Learn it first, then bring it as a backup! As you get more advanced, you can learn primitive fire-starting that doesn't require any of these, like using a hand drill, fire plow, fire piston, or bow drill.

**Navigation:** Plain and simple, you need to know where you're going. It doesn't matter whether you're walking down a path or crossing a mountain. Never just rely on a map saved on your phone. A nice waterproof map with a compass could really save your life.

**First aid:** There is no point in bringing a full first aid kit if you don't know how to use it. However, a first aid kit can really save you in an emergency. Bare minimum, you should have something to wrap around a wound if you do unexpectedly get a large cut. A bandage works wonders for that in the field. Sure, you could cut your shirt, but then you don't have a shirt anymore!

**Backpack:** I can't imagine you'd take all your supplies in your pockets, so this probably seems pretty obvious. You need a pack. But, with so many bags out there to bring, where do you start? This is where you get to wander down to the local outfitter and figure out what suits your style, and your needs. Just don't get hung up on all the fancy (and often pricey) gear. When you're starting, go simple. Find something that fits the basic kit above and head out!

# The Rule of Threes

Trivia time! What is the most important thing to do in a survival situation? I'll give you a hint, it's not related to calling for help on your cell phone—but, boy oh boy, would that save you if you had some cell reception. Plus, let's face it, if that's available, use it.

I'm talking about basic Survival 101 here. Deciding what you can and should do often comes down to priorities. The Rule of Threes is something that is taught by instructors around the world and is a good way to start thinking about what's really important if you're stranded in the woods. It goes something like this.

You can live about three minutes without oxygen.

You can last three hours without proper warmth and shelter.

You can survive only about three days without water.

You can survive three weeks without food.

You can survive three months without rescue or human interaction.

Let's also remember this is more of a guideline than hard-and-fast rules. Anyone who's ever looked up the world record breath hold will know it's far longer than three minutes. Plus, if you're walking around on a nice fall day somewhere, you can go way more than three to four hours without a shelter to protect you from the elements.

The point of this is that it makes you prioritize what you're going to do first. The first thing is to always make some shelter and a warm place to be. Then look for water. Only after that is taken care of should you start finding food. Believe it or not, that is one of the last things you should worry about.

Now, let's go into each in more detail, just in case you're really curious.

# Three Minutes without Air

Currently, the world record breath hold is over twenty-two minutes. However, when you hold your breath, there is still oxygen circulating through your blood to your brain. But, if that stops, you're in trouble. Within 30 to 180 seconds of oxygen deprivation to the brain, you'll lose consciousness. At about 60 seconds, your brain cells start to die. At three minutes, neurons suffer more extensive damage, and long-term problems really become likely. At ten minutes, even if the brain is alive, lasting brain damage is almost a certainty. At fifteen minutes, it's almost impossible to survive. However, some of this changes with cold.

For example, people have been retrieved from cold-water near-drowning accidents forty minutes after the incident and have recovered without brain damage. This is because cold temperatures slow the heartbeat. The body responds by also redistributing the blood flow toward the organs that need most of the blood and oxygen: the heart, lungs, and brain.

# Three Hours without Shelter

The Rule of Threes states that you can survive for three hours without shelter. But how long do you think you can survive in an icy cold lake before you lose consciousness? The answer, according to Minnesota doctors, is only around fifteen to thirty minutes, depending on just how cold it is. I present this because it may be the extreme situation here. It seems to break the rule.

If instead you're in a comfortable seventy-degree location, you're likely to have all the time you need. Still, the importance of shelter is that you need to keep your body temperature up so that you can perform the other important tasks, like getting water, food, and rescue.

# Three Days without Water

Water makes up 60 percent of an individual's weight, and losing as much as 3 percent of that weight in water will lead to dehydration.

And dehydration is what we're really worried about when we don't have water. Dehydration can happen quickly. That causes you to get thirsty, which can cause sluggishness and fatigue. In the end, it will result in organ failure and death.

So if you ask how long the average person can last without water, the answer is about three days. The following factors, however, will change this slightly.

- 🔥 The person's age
- 🔥 How active they are
- 🔥 Their overall health
- 🔥 Their body type—height and weight
- 🔥 Their sex
- 🔥 Environmental factors, like the characteristics of deserts or Arctic tundra

Don't forget that drinking pure stream water isn't the only way you can rehydrate yourself. Many foods are great at rehydrating your body. Fruits, berries, and veggies, for instance, are fantastic. Stay away from extremely salty foods because they'll actually dehydrate you more. That also means, don't drink saltwater!

# The Perfect Knife

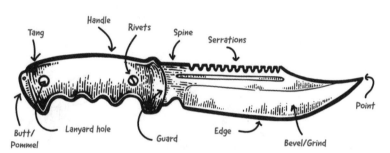

Tang

Handle

Rivets

Spine

Serrations

Point

Butt/
Pommel

Lanyard hole

Guard

Edge

Bevel/Grind

# Your Literal Lifeline: Rope

# Different Types of Rope

There are many different types of rope (sometimes called cordage) that you can purchase. Each rope type has slightly different properties. Here are a few you might come across.

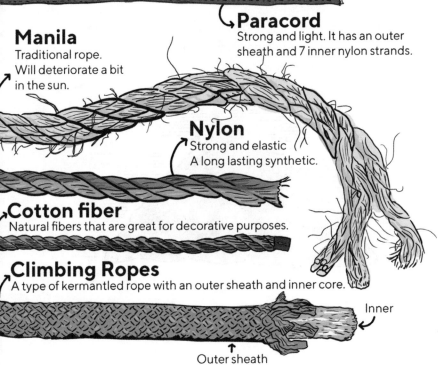

**Paracord**
Strong and light. It has an outer sheath and 7 inner nylon strands.

**Manila**
Traditional rope. Will deteriorate a bit in the sun.

**Nylon**
Strong and elastic
A long lasting synthetic.

**Cotton fiber**
Natural fibers that are great for decorative purposes.

**Climbing Ropes**
A type of kermantled rope with an outer sheath and inner core.

Inner

↑
Outer sheath

# Basic Shelters

## Basic Debris Pile

A debris pile is the simplest and most basic form of survival shelter. If things are getting dark and you're lost and cold, this may be the best thing you can do.

# Lean-To Shelter

If the wind is coming mainly from one direction and you have some sort of larger structure element like a rock or fallen tree, you can create a simple lean-to shelter.

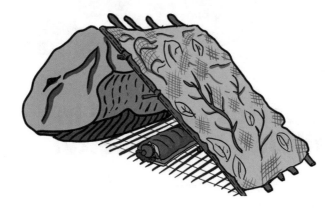

Lean a bunch of sticks up on one side. Cover the sticks with leaves, palm fronds, and other vegetation to protect yourself from the rain and to insulate the structure.

# Fallen Tree—A-Frame Shelter

Much like the lean-to, you'll stack sticks and debris around an existing structure. In this scenario, make extra sure that tree isn't going to fall on you.

# Scenarios to Avoid in Building Your Shelter

**On ground that's damp:** Damp ground means that water is draining into the area. It'll be colder and the risk of flooding is much higher.

**On a mountain or ridge** where you're exposed to the wind. Gusts can pick up quickly in these areas.

**In ravines where it looks like water might drain** in a storm. Flash floods can happen quickly. Plus, cold air generally falls into these areas and will make you colder.

# Morse Code

Not everyone is going to take the time to learn this, but if you're carrying this guide with you, you'll at least have the know-how to send a message!

Dots represent short taps. Bars indicate long taps.

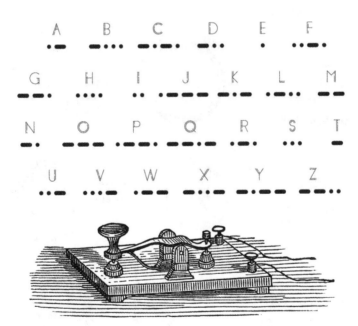

# Packing 101

I like to think of these items as an essential kit to survival should the unexpected happen.

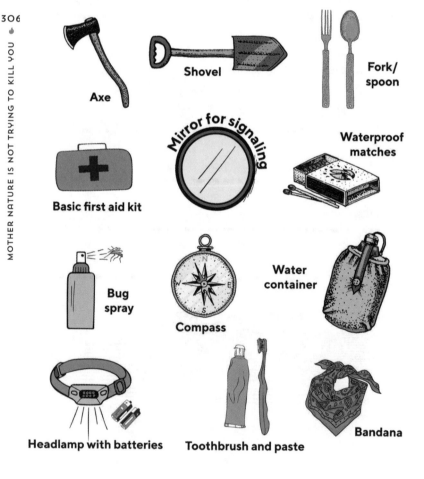

Axe

Shovel

Fork/spoon

Basic first aid kit

Mirror for signaling

Waterproof matches

Bug spray

Compass

Water container

Headlamp with batteries

Toothbrush and paste

Bandana

**Face mask**

**Sunglasses**

**Rain gear**

**Emergency sleeping bag**

**A whistle**

**Smartwool clothes**

**Fishing hooks/line**

**A few emergency meals to start things off**

**Hand sanitizers**

**Waterproof notebook and a pencil**

**A sturdy hiking pack to put it all in**

# Six Key Knots

### Clove Hitch

A clove hitch is two half-hitches tied around an object. It is a quick release knot and is particularly useful when the length of the running end needs to be adjusted. It does hold tight when one strand is weighted. It's often used in climbing situations because it can be tied with one hand and untied easily. Be aware that it's not a great knot to tie around square posts as it is prone to some slippage.

## Bowline

The bowline is one of the first knots people learn, often with the phrase, "Rabbit comes out of the hole, goes around the tree and back down the hole." It's useful in creating a loop at the end of a rope and is pretty easy to untie.

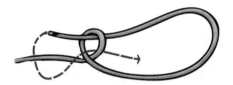

## Trucker's Hitch

The trucker's hitch is useful in tying downloads and getting the rope really tight. This is because of the way the initial loop acts a bit like a pulley and allows you to pull the whole thing tight. Essentially you tie a slip knot halfway up the rope. The remaining rope is tied around an anchor point, threaded back through the slip knot and pulled tight. This provides mechanical advantage for pulling it tight—much like a pulley system. Any knot, such as two half-hitches, can then be used to secure it.

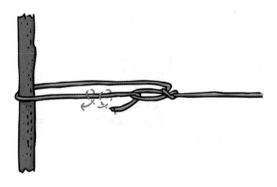

## Taut Line

The taut-line hitch is an adjustable loop knot that can be used for lines under tension. It comes in handy when the line needs to be adjusted to maintain tension. Some possible uses include tying down a tent tarp line or tent stake. Care should be given not to tie this knot around you as it could easily constrict tightly.

## Alpine Butterfly

This is a type of mid-line knot. This is a great knot for mountaineering situations where you want to tie someone into the middle of the rope. That's because it will take loading in three directions. It's also easy to untie after a load has been removed from it.

## Double Figure-Eight Knot

This is the essential climbing knot, so I'm including it here. It's a great stopper knot if tied as a single knot. One figure-eight is often tied, then looped around a climbing harness and threaded back on itself to make the double figure-eight. This knot will not come undone and is the industry standard for tying yourself into a rope that you want to trust your life on.

# Appendix:
# A Few Lists

# Strongest Bites

1. Nile croc: 5,000 psi

2. Saltwater croc: 3,700 psi

3. American alligator: 1,800 psi

4. Hippopotamus: 1,800 psi

5. Jaguar: 1,500 psi

6. Bull shark: 1,3500 psi

7. Gorilla: 1,300 psi

8. Polar bear: 1,200 psi

9. Grizzly: 1,160 psi

10. Hyena: 1,100 psi

# Largest Land Carnivores (Recorded Largest Weight)

1. Brown bear—2,400 pounds

2. Polar bear—2,209 pounds

3. American black bear—1,102 pounds

4. Asiatic black bear—800 pounds

5. Tiger—714 pounds

6. Lion—690 pounds in the wild

7. Spectacled bear—441 pounds

8. Sloth bear—423 pounds

9. Jaguar—353 pounds

10. Giant panda—353 pounds

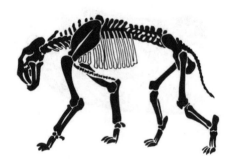

# Largest Land Animals

1. African elephant—24,000 pounds

2. Asian elephant—15,400 pounds

3. African forest elephant—13,200 pounds

4. White rhino—9,910 pounds

5. Hippo—9,900 pounds

6. Indian rhino—8,800 pounds

7. Black rhino—6,400 pounds

8. Javan rhino—5,000 pounds

9. Giraffe—4,400 pounds

10. Gaur—3,300 pounds

# Biggest Whales

1. Blue whale—98 feet/173 tons

2. Fin whale—90 feet/72 tons

3. Sperm whale—67 feet/56 tons

4. Right whale—60 feet/100 tons

5. Bowhead whale—59 feet/100 tons

6. Humpback whale—52 feet/30 tons

7. Sei whale—50 feet/28 tons

8. Gray whale—49 feet/36 tons

9. Bryde's whale—46 feet/25 tons

10. Minke whale—35 feet/11 tons

# Africa's Ten Most Dangerous Animals

The deadliest animal is the one that just killed you, so I'm lumping all ten into one list without trying to say which is deadlier. I added humans to remind you that we're part of this too.

- 🔥 African buffalo
- 🔥 Black rhino
- 🔥 Black mamba
- 🔥 Elephant
- 🔥 Hippo
- 🔥 Humans
- 🔥 Lion
- 🔥 Mosquitoes (that carry parasites)
- 🔥 Nile crocodile
- 🔥 Puff adder

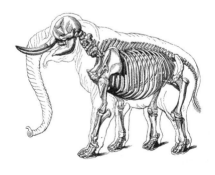

# Contributors (via Review)

We want to thank the following scientists for their review of the book. Their knowledge made the entire book better.

Gaelin Rosenwaks
Global Ocean Exploration

Dustin Smith
Curator of Herpetology, North Carolina Zoo

David Bodenham
Applied Ecologist, Eco Sapien

Dr. Roland Kays
Zoologist, NC State University, NC Museum of Natural Sciences

Jim Brady
Science Editor

Jesús A. Rivas, PhD
Herpetologist, New Mexico Highlands University

Kenneth Catania, PhD
Biologist, Vanderbilt University

Damien Caillaud, PhD
Behavioral Ecologist, UC Davis

Shauhin Alavi, PhD
Evolutionary Anthropologist, Max Planck Inst of
Animal Behavior

John J. Mayer, PhD
Savannah River National Laboratory

Christina Zedenck, PhD
Herpetologist, University of Brisbane

Nick Whitney, PhD
Shark Biologist, New England Aquarium

Chris Morgan
Wildlife Ecologist

Jamie Seymour, PhD
James Cook University

Casey Parker, PhD
Entomologist, University of Florida

Jim Brady
Science Review

**I would also like to thank the following for their mental and fiscal support of this book:**

Matthias Metzger, Jeff Osborne, Tomas Huntley, James Green, Morgan Price, Anja Landsmann, Johanna van de Woestijne.

**I'd also like to thank these amazing science enthusiasts for their continued support of our work:**

Lu Musetti, Leigh Allen, Neil Gonzalez, Elaine Franklin, Charles Rice, Richard Burguillos, Amy Sauls, Keith Sparkjoy, Laura Le, Stephanie Castillo, Tim, Susan Haines, Dylan Bailly, John Kuentz, Borian Bruckner, Mike Chimneyswift, Kate Rose, Alex

Dainis, The Wild Lens, Elisabet Brock, Sean, Larry Nelson, Jennifer Hungerford, Maureen Olivier, Shannon Richardson, Christopher Borgatti, Adrian Smith, Christa Dillworth, Daniella Ellingson, Adam Hallihan, Lauren Burn, Michelle Lotcker, Anne Chamberlain, Cindy Schneider, Karen Origlio, Stefanie Beutler, Hannah Reynolds, Jonas Stenstrom, Dustin Growick, Holly D'Oench, Tobias Haase, Dexter Henry, Ashley Grice, Vanessa Hill, Damon Gochneaur, Zak Martellucci,Karen Origlio, Alison Paylor, Ron Stafford, Mike Sigers, Corey Nixon, Robin Bare Swindle, Glenn Skaggs, Isa Betancourt, Michael Girard, Rhys Paine, Amos Voltz, Lori Bodine, Rochelle Jones, Summer Kern, Kerry Alfred, Marc and Judy, Peter Hansen, Tino H. A. Bratbo, Gregorio Forondajr, Scott Aughe, Cheri Amarna, Janelle Anderson, Ronald Mcmullen, Gaby Bastyra, Hannah Walker, and Michael Van Durme.

# About the Authors

**Rob Nelson** is a biologist and an Emmy award-winning TV host. He's most known for his work as an online educator via UntamedScience.com and StoneAgeman.com. He's famous for hosting the popular Science Channel series Secrets of the Underground, Animal Planet's *Life After Chernobyl* and Discovery Channels *Man Eating Python*. He also hosted and produced the popular Untamed Science series which is in half the classrooms in the United States. Rob now leads classes with his family via *StoneAgeMan* where they teach bushcraft and outdoor knowledge. Rob also authored a book on science filmmaking for people trying to better communicate science in media.

**Haley Chamberlain Nelson** is a science host on television and online. She has been a writer, producer, and host with *StoneAgeMan* and *Untamed Science* for over ten years, making science content viewed by over half the classrooms in the US and over 100,000 views per month online. She is driven by the intersection of science and the arts, finding ways to creatively explore and share the natural world. Her happy place is doing this work and play as a family with her two sons and husband. She also really loves sneakers. Her most recent credits include Smithsonian Channel's hit series *Bug Bites,* four years hosting JASON Live! Events, and six seasons of Science Channel's *What On Earth?* She co-wrote the award-winning documentary *Decoding the Driftless,* currently gaining acclaim on the festival circuit and winning Best Picture in the Los Angeles International Film Festival.

Mango Publishing, established in 2014, publishes an eclectic list of books by diverse authors—both new and established voices—on topics ranging from business, personal growth, women's empowerment, LGBTQ studies, health, and spirituality to history, popular culture, time management, decluttering, lifestyle, mental wellness, aging, and sustainable living. We were recently named 2019 *and* 2020's #1 fastest growing independent publisher by *Publishers Weekly*. Our success is driven by our main goal, which is to publish high quality books that will entertain readers as well as make a positive difference in their lives.

Our readers are our most important resource; we value your input, suggestions, and ideas. We'd love to hear from you—after all, we are publishing books for you!

Please stay in touch with us and follow us at:

Facebook: Mango Publishing
Twitter: @MangoPublishing
Instagram: @MangoPublishing
LinkedIn: Mango Publishing
Pinterest: Mango Publishing
Newsletter: www.mangopublishinggroup.com/newsletter

Sign up for our newsletter at and receive a free book!

Join us on Mango's journey to reinvent publishing, one book at a time.